Contents

Part Two *The Creative Organization*

CORE QUALITIES

Core Qualities
A Gateway to
Human Resources

Daniel Ofman

SCRIPTUM MANAGEMENT

Published by
Scriptum Publishers
Dam 2
3111 BD Schiedam
The Netherlands

Tel: +31-10-427.10.22 Fax: +31-10-473.66.25
e-mail: info@scriptum.nl

This publication is designed to provide accurate and authoritative information in regard to the subject matter covered. It is sold with the understanding that the publisher is not engaged in rendering professional services. If professional advice or other expert assistance is required, the services of a competent professional person should be sought.

ISBN 90 5594 240 5   NUGI 684 – Management

*For Ines,
who helped me
come alive*

Don't ask yourself what the world needs.
Ask yourself what makes you come alive,
and go do that.
Because what the world needs
is people who have come alive.
HOWARD THURMON, minister

¹] Introduction

Do not go gentle into that good night,
Old age should burn and rave at close of day;
Rage, rage against the dying of the light.
DYLAN THOMAS

The Shifting Paradigm

How does a manager create an organization in which those he supervises take responsibility for their own (professional) lives, behave as part of the larger whole, act on the basis of their own core qualities and accomplish what (they say) they want?

Some cultures consider it more of an art to ask the right questions than to find the right answers, and these cultures particularly respect people for the quality of their questions. The answers are considered less important, because it is recognized that there are no unequivocal answers.

The longer I consider the question stated above, the clearer it becomes that the answer is both simple and difficult to realize. This has to do with leadership "from inside," with management from the core, with what could be described as "unifying leadership," which was the working title of this book for a long time during its writing: *Unifying Leadership: The Way to a Creative Organization,* which explains in one sentence what this book is about. For a while, I considered using "A crusade against powerlessness" as a subtitle. However, a crusade is rather reactive and primarily conducted against something, whereas the essential message of this book encourages being *creative* instead of *reactive.*

I get worked up about powerlessness, I cannot stand it. I get chills of frustration, seeing how many people at all levels within an organization feel powerless and incapable of exerting any influence on their situation. The amount of creative energy lost in this way is phenomenal. What a terrible waste!

During the past few years, environmental awareness has increased considerably. Things that were inconceivable 10 years ago are normal today, and it looks as if this positive development will continue for the time being. I think now is the time to pay some attention to our *inner environment,* to what is going on in our hearts and in our heads. How do we use our core qualities? How do we inspire ourselves and others? Why do we do things we do not really want to do? To what extent are we aware of our darker side? What do we really want to achieve? And so on.

Besides the concept of "inner environment," I would not be surprised at all if, within 10 years, the term *socio-environmental* pollution becomes an established expression, one used to measure the impact of an organization on the families of its employees. Every day, I am struck by how many people (particularly men) believe deep down that they do not devote enough time to their families, because they throw themselves into their work "wholeheartedly." Our obsession with achieving results is getting inhuman at times. I refuse to believe that this is the price we have to pay for prosperity. Looking at the human energy wasted in organizations, I believe we could accomplish more with less energy. This, however, requires effort, a kind of reflective "effort" that will make us focus on our inner world.

In this context something must be said about underlying principles or, in more complex terms, the underlying paradigm. Paradigm here is a definition of reality ("This is the way the world works…"). It is the set of basic principles underlying everybody's actions. Consciously or not, everyone acts and thinks according to a definition of reality or a paradigm. We need a paradigm to enable us to explain events in our lives and to give meaning to these events.

So far, history has gone through a number of paradigm shifts. These are caused by expansion of insight and consciousness, which has a snowball effect. One such paradigm shift began with the Polish astronomer Nicolaus Copernicus (1473–1543). In his case, the "heaven-shaking" change was caused, not so much by his assuming the existence of a heliocentric solar system—a concept that had been formulated centuries before—but the fact that he put inquiry and ratio before the Bible, thus rejecting *authority as a source of truth.* From that moment, the Church (read: authority) would be questioned fundamentally, and thirty or forty years later (despite limited means of communication) the world had changed complete-ly and *would never be the same.*

The Italian natural philosopher, astronomer and mathematician Gali-leo (1564–1642) added his bit to these developments with his far-reaching and dramatic dictum that science should confine itself to what can be measured. Until the end of the Middle Ages, the aim of science had always been to understand the purpose and the meaning of things. Suddenly, many things were no longer considered science: experience, intuition, intention and taste were all placed outside the pale of scientific thinking in one fell swoop.

The English philosopher, essayist, and statesman Francis Bacon (1561–1626) went even further, declaring that the aim of science was to subject nature. This shows how much scientific attitudes had changed in the course of a few centuries. Science no longer attempted to give purpose and meaning to phenomena, but from then on strove to wrest knowledge of these phenomena from nature. Nature was to be laid open and dis-sected; the earth was no longer the "nurturing mother," but something to be subjected and controlled.

With English mathematician and natural philosopher Isaac Newton (1643–1727) another shift of paradigm occurred. It was not his discovery of the law of gravity that was important (after all, this did not change the world this law operated in), but rather the fact that laws could be deduced from studying the world. This opened up a new perspective: the possibility of *constructing* the world. Once you know how something works, you can direct and control it. It was this concept that made its influence felt in the farthest corners of our world and thinking.

The paradigm currently dominant is still based on the assumption that the world is controllable (and can be constructed) from outside, that stasis is normal, that the world consists of disconnected components, and that everyone and everything is separate. Coherence must therefore be intro-duced from outside, because it does not exist naturally (paradigm A).

The implications of this paradigm are many. If I experience myself as separate from the rest of the world, it means that stealing a bicycle, polluting the environment or saying hello to someone will primarily be something I do to *others* and not so much to *myself.* If I (deliberately) harm others, this does not necessarily mean I also harm myself. Whether I subsequently approve or reject this does not change my feeling of separateness. My experiences, and therefore my actions, are determined by this "I-versus-you-thinking." This perspective explains why individuals tend to take better care of themselves than they do of their surroundings. Looking at how people treat themselves and their environment, we can only conclude that the great majority experience themselves as separate from others. This is as true for organizations as for society as a whole.

From this perspective man is a "skin-encapsulated ego."[1] Everything inside his skin is "I," everything outside is "not I." Although biologically correct, this is not the whole truth. Many of today's problems ensue from this paradigm. At the organizational level, this "we-versus-them-thinking" is recognizable in the struggle between levels, departments, organizations and even between organizations and customers.

If I assume that stasis is normal, then movement and change become abnormal, threatening and to be avoided. For a manager, this may mean that he expects people to object to change (and believes it normal for them to object) and that he considers the exercise of visible power an ordinary and proper way to realize the desired results. *He* has to do it, and it takes power and strength to get others to do something for you. This strength is usually sought in displays of visible strength, by stimulating action and "doing things." Power is sought by trying to keep matters *controllable* with instrumental means (such as planning systems and motivational techniques).[2] In this process, attention is always focused outside, on others.

In established medical science, disease is still considered a matter of "defective components" of the body. Once the defective component has been found, it can be repaired or replaced. It is very much the question whether this mechanical cause-and-effect way of thinking will provide solutions to diseases like cancer and AIDS, as these may be diseases not of parts of the body, but of the whole organism, and may require a different way of thinking.

At present a new paradigm is developing, which is based on the idea that everyone and everything is connected to everyone and everything else and that movement is normal.[3] In this paradigm, every individual is considered the creator of his or her present and future reality. People are responsible for themselves, and there is no room for chance, power-lessness or meaninglessness. Motivation comes from inside you, and there is no division between inside and outside; the world is an integrated whole, constantly changing, a stream of events mutually influencing each other (paradigm B).

From this perspective, people experience the world differently, both in their private lives and at work. What you do to others, you do to yourself. Stealing from others is stealing from yourself. Polluting the environment is polluting yourself. Saying hello to someone else is saying hello to yourself. It is what Cees Swarttouw calls "inclusiveness." "To be inclusive with some-one" means "to be connected" and not experience yourself as separate.

A manager working with this paradigm will try to focus rather than control energy. He will present his vision and look for ways to address people's creativity and sense of responsibility (as individuals within a larger whole). Resistance is then not something to be avoided or over-come, but a meaningful part of the process of continual change, and a phenomenon that should be regarded as a signal. The important thing is not to get from X to Y, but to keep asking on the way whether Y is still where you want to go, and whether Z would not be more suitable in view of the changing reality… etc. He will mainly be concerned with *connec-tions*, with the *process*, the release and focalization of *energy*, and with directional leadership. You could call him a "focalizer."[4]

It is not just that our paradigm colors our interpretation of what we see, but that even our perceptions are determined by the paradigm we adopt, because we only want to see what confirms our definition of reality. As a result, our basic principles are not confirmed by what we see, but we ourselves confirm our basic principles by perceiving things in a certain way. This goes for both paradigms described above.

This book is based on paradigm B, which treats organizations as living organisms that have both internal and external tasks to fulfil, tasks that require an organic and respectful approach aimed at healthy growth and healing (becoming whole). Healthy organisms are characterized by rhythm and balance, and have room for expansion and contraction, for exhaling and inhaling. This is true of both individuals and developing organizations.

Healthy organisms are vital and aligned. *Vitality* ensues from attention and care for primary (work) processes. Within the organization this manifests itself in working on relations and connections between people, departments and levels; externally, it entails maintaining the relationship between the company and the client. *Alignment* occurs when people behave as parts of an integrated whole and combine their energy.

In my opinion, success and growth are no longer measured by financial and economic results alone; ultimately, this concerns growth of consciousness. The new consciousness is based on *abundance* and *reciprocity*. In this system, money is a manifestation of life energy. The way people deal with money clearly indicates how they deal with their life energy. Money is at least as important now as in the "old days" but in a different way. Declining profits are a signal something is wrong with the energy, that giving and receiving are out of balance and that reciprocity has been disturbed.

Soul, Values, Mission and Vision

Considering it from the above point of view, an organization is not just an organism, it is a spiritual entity with a soul. An organization's soul is sometimes visible and tangible, in which case we speak of "spirit" or vigor. It radiates life force and is a source of enormous energy. It generates enthusiasm, is infectious and animates all levels of an organization. It inspires. In an organization's soul or core is its identity, its *mission* and *talent*. This comprises the reason for its existence.

Soul is very difficult to describe, it must be experienced. A manager's task is to create the circumstances in which people can be inspired.

The people, and especially the management, of an inspired organization are aware of:

• History	Where we come from
• Values	What is the basis of our thinking
• Mission	Why do we exist
• Vision	Where are we going
• Energy	What makes us "move"
• Structure	Which channels this energy
• Resources	By which we realize goals
• Culture	We live in and create

In a healthy, inspired organization, the soul is perceptible in the respect the organization has for its *history* and existing *values*. The soul is visible in the *mission* and the *vision* the organization is working towards and in the way human energy is being mobilized. The *structure* that has been created (to harness this energy) and the way people and *resources* are employed within this structure also contribute to the manifestation of the soul. Finally, an inspired organization will have an appreciable image, both internally and externally, due to its clearly recognizable organizational *culture*.

Traditionally, many managers have considered structuring or restructuring systems to ensure optimum efficiency in the employment of people and resources as one of their main tasks. In the above model these are the "lowest" and "final" two levels. It strikes me that history is more or less taken into account when organizations are (re)structured, but that there is too little explicit consideration of background, values, mission, vision, energy and culture.

What are values and what are mission and vision? Values, and an organization's mission and vision that are derived from them, provide answers to questions of meaning. Inner values motivate people from inside. For example, if one of your values is to provide quality, this will

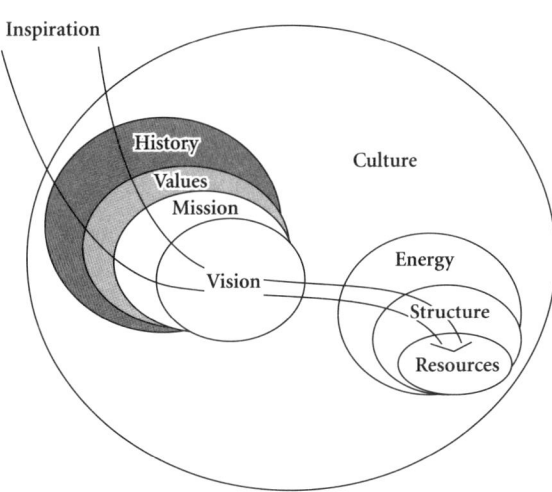

The Inspired Organization

influence everything you do. The values in an organization are what finally determine its identity and individuality. If aesthetic beauty is an important value in an organization, product design will play an important role in the process of product development. The design department of such a company will receive more and higher quality attention than that of a company lacking this value. Its values will compel an organization to make a contribution. What this will be is established in a mission, like the one formulated by Harley Davidson: "Our purpose is to create an atmosphere which affords individuals the opportunity to reach their maximum growth potential."

There is something inevitable, something *obligatory* about the mission statements of some organizations, which lends the mission a compulsory air, while the idea is for a mission to ensue from a *free will* to contribute to the larger whole. Such "mission statements" reflect little of this desire to contribute and free choice. If a "mission statement" mentions gaining a 26 percent market share, wanting to be market leader or to be technologically "the best" this, in my opinion, has little to do with an organization's mission and talent. The mission has been reduced to formulating quantitative goals or means. At best, it is an "embellished" objective, which means that contact with the organization's soul has been lost; the channel has been blocked so to speak. Eventually, this will manifest itself in a lack of inspiration and vitality in the organization, and sometimes in obsessiveness. If a lot of very hard work is done in these organizations—which is often the case—it is usually done for personal gain; the prevalent mentality tends to be "compete and beat."

A vision is an image of what is being created; it is a potential reality and always directed towards the future.

A vision is	A vision provides
Feasible	Focus
Authentic	Enthusiasm
Enriching	Meaning
Inspiring	Commitment
Directed towards the future	Creative tension

Vision mobilizes and focuses energy. Without vision, organizations tend to become fragmented and fall apart. Vision determines the direction of the energy, and by focussing the energy of individuals, it is complemented and reinforced.

If forces (energy) are not focussed, organizations tend to waste energy, because they keep having to pay too much attention to mutual adjustment. Organizations without vision end up calling many problems communication problems. By doing this, they consider the cause determined and go back to "business as usual," until a few months later, when the same diagnosis is repeated. The argument explaining why nothing is actually done about it is well-known: people do not want to get bogged down in endless meetings and paperwork. The question is why so much attention and energy is taken up by adjusting to one another. The answer is obvious, to me, anyway: *Without a mission, a vision and focussed energy, every question, every daily problem, every situation is a confrontation with the fact that there is no sense of collectivity.*

If things are as they should be, an organization's current vision will be anchored in the past and *rooted* in norms and values. Many organizational problems can be traced back to differences in values and vision. Any lack of clarity concerning this will sooner or later be manifested in systems, procedures and regulations.

Financial systems clearly reflect the values of an organization. For example, in our own consultancy (Kern Konsult) we pay a great deal of attention to the handling of financial matters. We make a distinction between two aspects when determining the fees for a day's work:

- The first question is: what is proper for a client to pay?
- The second question is: what is proper for us (as a firm) to receive of this?

Propriety has most to do with what is "proper" for the client to pay to receive what we offer. If our fee is too low, the client is sold short. He cannot receive, because he does not give enough. If the rate is too high, the client is also sold short because we ask too much. If the rate is right, you create a reciprocal relationship.

In practice, the fees for a day's work are fairly high, because we think we have a lot to offer. Whether it is "proper" for us to get all that money is a completely different question. For this reason, we devote a third of our profits to financing initiatives that do not directly benefit us. These may be donations, loans, sponsoring initiatives, publication of articles on socially relevant subjects etc. This "initiatives fund" also expresses our belief in abundance. We believe that "shortage consciousness" ("There is never enough") actually creates shortages, whereas "abundance consciousness" creates abundance.

In practical terms this implies that on the one hand, we do not negotiate about fees, and on the other that a job is stopped because of the fee we request. Money is an expression of life energy and the way people treat money is a reflection of the values within the organization.

Just as a third goes into the initiatives fund, a third also goes to our employees in profit sharing, as an expression of our principles of entrepreneurship and personal responsibility.

Appendix 2, "Kern Konsult's Genetic Code," contains the identity, values and direction of our firm.

Energy and Structure

Energy is the fuel we need to finally take action, that moves us. In other words: energy *fills* and *forms* a structure. Before structuring an organization, it is important to consider the way in which its management wants to release and focus the energy present in the organization. These choices determine subsequent structuring possibilities. Underlying a hierarchical top-down structure is an implicit assumption about the way energy is to be released, namely from the top down. The choice of a network structure is based on a different principle regarding the harnessing of energy, by stimulating, rewarding and respecting personal initiative and responsibility.

The model of the inspired organization introduced above, which is an extension of Robert Terry's[5] Diamond Model, shows that the structure determines how people and resources are (or can be) employed. Vice versa, the opportunities for structuring are to some extent restricted by the people and resources available, while the chosen structure limits the possibilities of releasing energy etc.

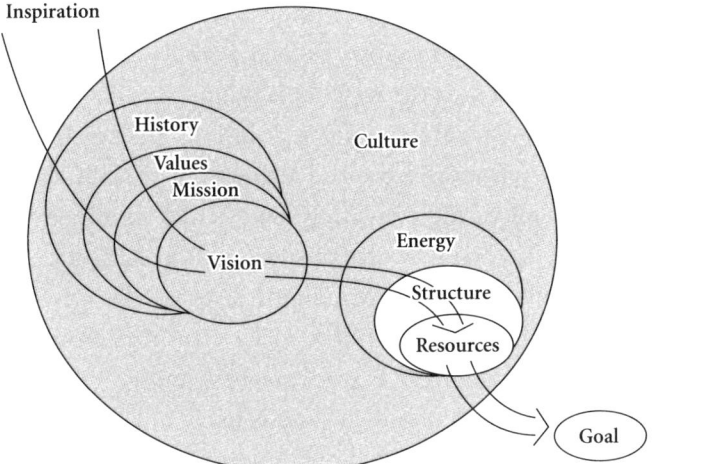

The Traditional View on Organizing

I believe it is time to adjust our thinking on the nature of organizations and organizing. According to traditional organizational theory, to organize is to manage people and resources for realizing a certain goal.[6] Actually, this is only a small part of the model of the inspired organization.

In my opinion, organizing is establishing, creating and keeping clean the energy channels through which energy can flow and inspire people to realize the organization's vision.

Examining the concept of organization from this point of view, I consider myself, as organization consultant, also a chimney sweep, acupuncturist, midwife, guide and (process) architect.

Management from Inside

Unifying management means "management from inside," which implies that a manager cannot stay on the sidelines. It is no longer a matter of management techniques or skill, it is all about *developing consciousness,* which is an inner process: unfolding the layers in which our consciousness is wrapped.

The traditional paradigm will not really be much support in this process of developing consciousness, because it approaches thinking and doing mainly as outward-directed activities that are directed at making things manageable, getting them under control, wanting to change or fight them or make them grow (both materially and financially). This outward-directedness causes us to look mainly outside the self for causes of events, phenomena and problems. Solutions are largely sought in the application of even more advanced technology or skills, with reorganization and restructuring providing (ostensible) solutions to problems that lie much deeper and concern the way we think and look at things.

Reflection on underlying paradigms is especially important today, because we are in the middle of a social transition from paradigm A (separateness) to paradigm B (inclusiveness and connectedness). This transition will not pass unnoticed and is likely to lead to drastic (structural) changes in many organizations. Environmental problems and technological developments will play a major role in these changes, because computer networks and satellite TV are turning the world into one big network of mutually influential connections from which there is no escape for countries, organizations, groups, and individuals. Mutual dependence and interconnectedness have by now become so encompassing, that it is impossible for parts of the network to behave like isolated cells. If they do, they become cancer cells multiplying at the expense of the whole organism and causing tumors. They will eventually be rejected and die. This goes for all levels: world, nation, organization, group and individual.

If mankind as a whole persists in the separation of each individual from another, of its separation from the environment and the earth, I feel that the final result is predictable. The earth will "reject" mankind, or, as Gregory Bates dramatically puts it:

If this [Me-versus-You model] is your estimate of your relationship to nature and you have advanced technology, your likelihood of survival will be that of a snowball in hell. You will either die of toxic by-products of your own hate, or simply, over-population and overgrazing.

The purpose of this book is to provide some insights and tools that can contribute to the new management as it is currently developing. It in no way pretends to be complete, or even finished. It is a reflection of the discoveries I have made and the experience and insights I have gained over the past years.

How does a manager create an organization in which those he supervises take responsibility for their own (professional) lives, behave as parts of a larger whole, act on the basis of their core qualities and realize what (they say) they want?

These questions will be examined in more detail below.

Short Summary and Division into Chapters

Part One is about creative man and consists of three chapters. Chapter 2 is mostly about core qualities: what they are, how they can be recognized in yourself and others, and how they can be improved. Chapter 3 mainly concerns the individual creative process. Central themes are learning to handle the tension of making choices and how to make effective choices. Chapter 4 goes deeper into the question of who the real I is. It is useful to ask oneself who actually controls the inner self, particularly when the creative process does not develop according to expectation or plan.

Part Two deals with creative organizations and consists of four chapters. Chapter 5 is about the developing organization. It provides a number of bases for supervising processes of change as well as three angles for finding a basis. Chapter 6 deals with the creative organizational culture. Four ways to make the concept of culture more tangible are reviewed, and an indication is given of when to use which approach. Chapter 7 is about saying good-bye to the past. Transitions to new situations are seldom managed, because too much attention is paid to the new situation and not enough to the past. Chapter 8 describes the three stages of the development from a reactive via a responsive to a creative organization.

In Part Three, we re-examine a number of themes from the perspective of the creative organization. Chapter 9 takes a closer look at project work. The new paradigms treat this as a way of collectivizing the individual creative process. In Chapter 10 we take a closer look at quality. Quality is essentially an expression of Love, which can sometimes be at odds with your ability to consistently satisfy clients' expectations. Chapter 11 reconsiders Creativity. Enhancing the capacity for creative problem solving is primarily a matter of learning to think differently (in terms of possibilities). Chapter 12 describes a reflective trip on a raft down the Colorado River and through the Grand Canyon. Appendix 1 includes the "Earth Charter." Appendix 2 contains Kern Konsult's Genetic Code.

Part One

Creative Man

God is a being
that knows good
without evil
as a point of reference.

²] Core Qualities

What you perceive in others
you are strengthening in yourself.
Course in Miracles

I N SOME CULTURES it easy to point out to yourself and to others what needs to be improved, what you are doing wrong, how things should be handled differently etc. This is something you learned at your mother's knee. As children coming home from school after your first test you said, full of enthusiasm: "Daddy, look! I only made two mistakes!" We did not mention the fact that we had twenty-eight correct answers, because that was not what was counted. You are supposed to make as few errors as possible. That is what you are judged by. No wonder we can immediately say what is wrong with others and ourselves. We have been very well trained in this.

In management it is important to consider what is right and going well. This is nothing new. For years, management literature has been written about the importance of showing appreciation for work well-done and giving people a pat on the back now and then. *The One Minute Manager* [1] explains how this can be done in one minute: by making eye contact with each other, touching people, etc. It is remarkable that motivation in such cases is considered as something brought about from outside by the manager. Motivation is nearly always in terms of others, about how to motivate others. Managers are regarded as "motivation machines" that can be taught—or rather programmed in—the best way to achieve this. It is hardly ever about the manager's desire and need for contact with himself and others.

According to the new paradigm, managers are particularly responsible for their own motivation and inspiration. They do not primarily try to motivate others, because they know that their best contribution is to get to know and inspire themselves and let themselves be inspired. The more a manager discovers about himself, the better he will be able to understand others and perform his role as coach or "facilitator," because he learned from personal experience what is necessary for further growth and development. His main responsibility is to take care of his own development. Among other things, self-knowledge means that a manager knows his strengths and core qualities. Besides awareness of his positive qualities, he should also have some insight into the distortions of his positive qualities. Learning to recognize qualities as such is not just useful for himself; groups, departments and organizations have core qualities too, and insight into them can be very illuminating.

Core Qualities

Core qualities are attributes that form part of a person's essence (core); people are steeped in these qualities, which place all their—more or less striking—characteristics in a certain light. A person is "colored" by his or her core qualities. It is their strong point, the characteristic that immediately comes to mind when we think of this person. Examples of core qualities are determination, consideration (for others), precision, courage, receptivity, orderliness, empathy, flexibility, etc. Core qualities are expressions of the Self that generate inspiration.[2] They are not so much characteristics as possibilities that can be "tuned in to." Just as radio sound quality is partly determined by fine-tuning it to the right wavelength, so a manager becomes more inspiring when he is tuned in to his own core qualities. And just as the capacity of the amplifier affects the final sound quality, so, too, does the creative capacity of a manager partly determine the impact he has on his surroundings.

Core qualities can be recognized as a person's special qualities, about which they themselves will say: "But everyone can do that!" Everyone cannot and what is more, if the underlying core quality were to be removed, the person would be unrecognizable. That is because all other, less prominent qualities are infused with this core quality. The core quality is *always* potentially present. It cannot be switched on and off at will, although it can be concealed. The main distinction between qualities and skills is that qualities come from inside and skills are acquired from outside. Skills can be learned; qualities can be developed.

The clearer the image we have of our core qualities, the more consciously we can apply them to our work. Someone whose core quality is, for example, perseverance, knows he or she will function particularly well in situations that require staying power, and that he/she will always be able to "hang in there," both at work and at home. Whether this principle will actually be applied in private life is another matter entirely.

Training and educational courses can teach managers certain skills that will enable them to function more effectively in different situations. For example, Situational Leadership according to Hersey and Blanchard[3] teaches how different situations demand different leadership styles. The following styles are distinguishable: Telling, Selling, Participating and Delegating.

This means that the manager must be both *flexible* and *effective* in his continuous redefinition of the appropriate leadership style. His flexibility allows him to adapt quickly to changing circumstances, while his effectiveness helps him always to choose the right style. It should be obvious that knowledge of the different leadership styles can be a valuable contribution to quicker insight into the requirements of every situation.

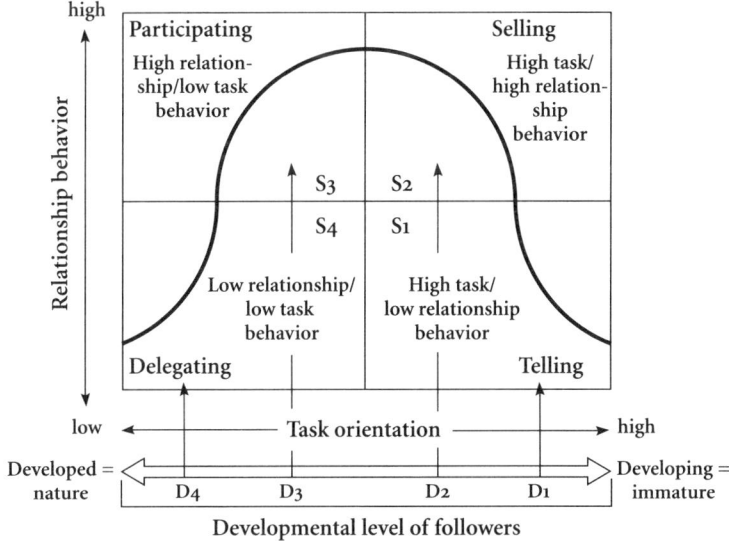

Situational Leadership according to Hersey & Blanchard

The question remaining is: *How* should this be done? How do I ensure that my style of leadership is flexible and effective? What is the best way to instruct, the most effective way to convince? And so on.

These questions can only be answered on the basis of self-knowledge, in other words, from an awareness of one's own specific core qualities. A leader whose core quality is perseverance will color the "telling" style of leadership with tenacity, while someone whose core quality is thoughtfulness will tint this style quite differently.

The more insight you have into your own core qualities and those of others, the easier it will be to integrate the different leadership styles into your own personality.

The better a style is adapted to the core quality, or in other words, the more fully the leadership style can be imbued with the core quality, the more credible and inspirational it will be. The effectiveness of a leadership style is primarily determined by the extent to which the person is himself and behaves authentically.

Core Quality and the Pitfall

Just as there is no light without darkness, there is also a light and a dark side to every core quality. The dark side is also called *distortion,* which is not the opposite of the core quality as active is the opposite of passive and strong the opposite of weak. Distortion is rather the result of an *overdeveloped* core quality. The core quality "helpfulness," for example, can become "interference," if overdeveloped and turned into a weakness instead of a strength.

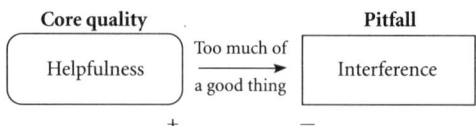

This is popularly called *"too much of a good thing,"* which expresses it perfectly. Someone who is too careful risks becoming fussy, and flexibility can easily go too far and be experienced by others as inconsistency, which is something a flexible person is likely to be accused of more than once.

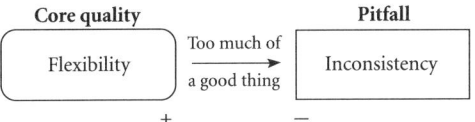

The distortion of someone's core quality is also his or her *"pitfall."* This pitfall is a label the person is often given by others. For example, a person whose core quality is decisiveness is reproached for being pushy.

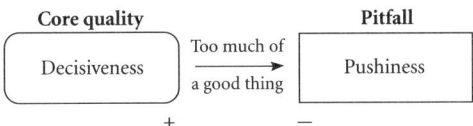

Whether or not this is right, the pitfall just goes with the core quality; they are inextricably bound. Core quality and pitfall go together like light and darkness. Facing the dark side of our core quality can be painful, especially if it appears that we are less perfect than our "idealized self-image" suggests. Learning to handle our core qualities and their distortions and becoming more aware of our positive inner potential is a process that, with the right intention, can be both instructive and fascinating.

From Pitfall to Core Qualities

Just as the distortion can be determined on the basis of the core quality, we can also return to the core quality from the distortion, although this is usually more difficult, especially if the distortion bothers people. It may be hard to imagine a positive core quality behind this distortion. Besides, we are not used to looking for positive things. For example, of what positive attribute is sentimentality the pitfall? It could be empathy, but there are also other possibilities.

If you do not know your core quality/qualities, there is only one way to discover it/them, and that is by asking yourself what people often reproach you for, in the sense of: "Don't be such a …" or "Don't be so …" Then ask yourself of what positive quality this is an excess, and there you have one of your core qualities.

Managers are confronted just as much with their employees' distortions as with their core qualities. Learning to spot the core qualities behind the distortions makes it easier to "see through" unpleasant behavior. The core quality of an "arrogant" person may be that he or she makes an impact. Obstinacy may hide the core quality of determination, just as Mr. X's obstinacy may be a distortion of his perseverance.

In confronting someone with his or her distortion, it is important to have a positive attitude to the person as a whole. Confrontation is only useful if it focuses on *behavior*. No one is ever a pushy, lazy or clingy person; rather, it is pushy, lazy or clingy behavior that bothers us. By separating person and behavior, it becomes easier to find the core quality behind negative behavior. If the one who initiates the confrontation has no desire to learn or confirm the other's core qualities, the confrontation will usually be ineffective and counterproductive. The confrontation will then be directed against, and not for the relation. It becomes only a matter of avoiding or destroying something instead of creating, shaping or realizing things! Confrontation only works in conjunction with the intention to make or restore contact.

Core Quality and the Challenge

Besides a pitfall, a person's core quality also comes with a "challenge." The challenge is the positive quality diametrically opposed to the pitfall. For example, the pitfall of pushiness may offer "patience" as a challenge.

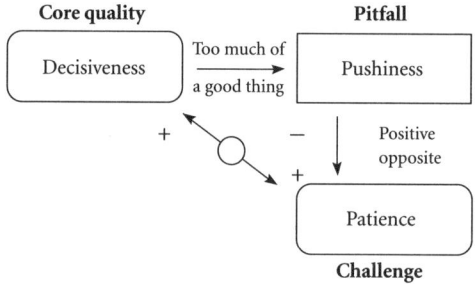

As the figure shows, the core quality and the challenge are *complementary* qualities. Striking the right *balance* between decisiveness and patience is what matters. Too much decisiveness can turn into pushiness, and to prevent the pitfall it is advisable to develop the challenge.

Creating balance means thinking in terms of *"and-and"* instead of *"either-or."* The secret is to be both decisive *and* patient at the same time. It is not a matter of becoming less decisive out of fear of being pushy, but to develop a patient decisiveness. Someone who is patiently decisive no longer runs a risk of being pushy, which is a logical consequence of his or her being "whole" in this respect. The problem is often to be able to see how the two qualities can be combined. It seems to be either a matter of decisiveness or patience. The person in question considers these qualities more as opposites than complements.

The pitfall of inconsistency may go with the challenges "orderliness" or "structure." Very likely, this person has great trouble imagining flexibility and orderliness as compatible instead of mutually exclusive concepts. "Yes, but then I'd become inflexible…" is a fairly standard reaction to suggestions along those lines. Inconsistency is no longer a problem for someone who is flexible in an orderly way.

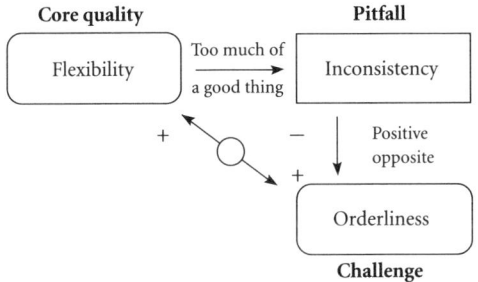

Pitfalls and challenges are usually the sources of conflicts a person has with his or her environment. Conflicts, irritation and mutual tension are often born of blindness to one's own qualities (and their distortions) and those of others.

Core Quality and the Allergy

As previously mentioned, potential conflicts with the environment can often be deduced from a person's core qualities. The problem is that the average person appears to be *allergic* to an excess of his or her challenge, particularly if personified in someone else.

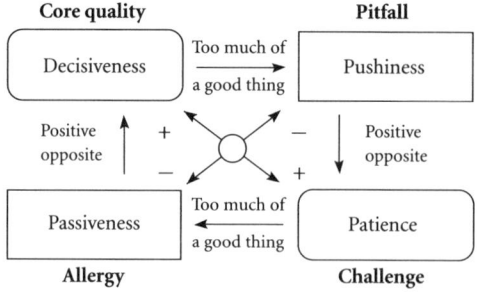

Decisive people will often blow their top if confronted with passivity in another. They are allergic to passivity, because it is an excess of their challenge (patience), and they often do not know how to handle it.

The more another confronts you with your own allergy, the greater your chance of falling into your pitfall. If your core quality is decisiveness, you run the risk of becoming even pushier, while reproaching the other person for being passive, etc. This can become a vicious circle which will be very hard to get out of without outside help. You risk reinforcing each other and ending up in a hopeless conflict.

In other words: look out for your pitfall when you spot your allergy in another. It is not their pitfall, but their allergy, that makes people most vulnerable, because this is what drives them into their pitfall.

When I let one of my friends read the first version of this book, he sent me a core quadrant he had been making about me over a glass of wine as a reaction to this chapter on core qualities. He found the chapter very clear but somewhat distant. He believed it should contain more examples, to enable the reader to better relate to it. He (rightly) concluded that I would probably have problems with this, since he had come to know me as someone who cannot stand ingratiation. Both to please the reader and not to avoid my challenge, I decided to add this example. And while I am typing this on my laptop, I keep feeling that I do not want to do this. Looking back over the last pages it seems I have said everything very nicely. So adding another quadrant—particularly one about myself—does seem ingratiating. Oh well, who ever said working on your challenge was easy … ?

Formulating the allergy completes the core quadrant. Now what happens if two similar characters meet? It is not hard to imagine that two

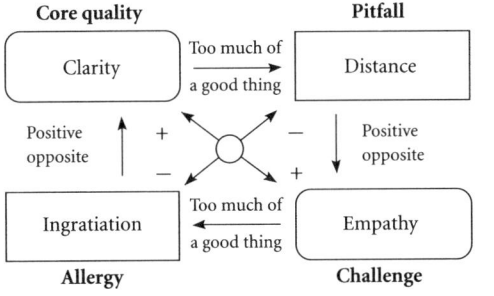

decisive persons may not have an easy time together. There is a very great risk such a meeting will turn into a confrontation between two very pushy types, which will be won by the stronger. The difference in confrontations between similar and contrasting characters is that, although a decisive person may have problems with someone who resembles him, he will respect the other. This is not the case for his opposite. If a "decisive" person encounters a "patient" person, he will soon label the patient person as "passive" and consequently look down on him or her. *Disdain* is characteristic of situations in which people are confronted with their allergies. Looking down on someone makes you vulnerable, because before you know it you will have fallen into your pitfall and cease to be effective.

The core quadrant makes it clear that a flexible person will have great difficulty recognizing "orderliness" in someone else as a positive quality and will tend to disqualify it by labeling it as "rigidity," because he or she cannot imagine orderliness and flexibility complementary to one another, neither in himself nor in others. Likewise, orderly people will find it difficult to appreciate flexibility in someone else, because they will immediately want to label it as "inconsistent or chaotic."

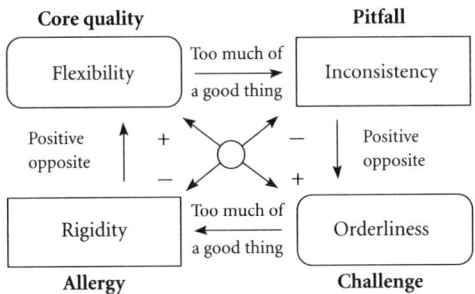

The core quadrant is not just a tool for discovering your own and others' core quality and challenge, it also demonstrates that it may very well be that a manager can learn most from the people he dislikes most (is allergic to) or, in other words:

Something you are allergic to in someone else is probably an excess of a quality you yourself need most. A manager can learn most (about himself) from those with whom he has the greatest problems interacting.

How to Approach the Core Quadrant

Core quadrants can be constructed from any of the four angles and checked in various ways. In some cultures people find the approach via the core quality the most difficult, partly due to the fact, already mentioned, that in some cultures it is unusual to say something positive about yourself. In such a culture it is much easier to criticize both yourself and others. This makes the second approach to the core quadrant easier. Most people can tell you exactly what they are regularly accused of, or what labels they are given, rightly or not, by other people. To find your pitfall, you only have to ask yourself what your partner pins on you regularly. The core quadrant can be completed using this approach.

The core quadrant can also be constructed further from a third approach: via the challenge. What quality would help you become a more balanced and more complete person? For many people, this question is not easy to answer either. It may be easier to ask yourself what quality you usually admire in others. This tends to be your challenge.

The fourth and simplest possibility for working out the core quadrant is through the allergy approach. Most people have no trouble pointing out what they cannot stand (in others). The last "angle" of the quadrant to be filled in can be double-checked, because its quality or distortion must correspond to the other three angles. Thus "indifference" must be considered as both an excess of "autonomy" and the (negative) opposite of "helpful," and the other extreme of "interference."

In fact, you can approach or judge each of the components of the quadrant in three different ways. It is always something that you say to or think about yourself; it is always something that you say to or think about others; it is always that others say to or think about you.

36

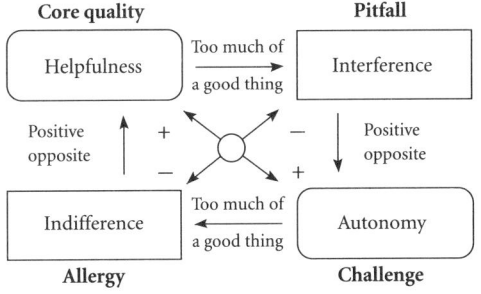

Thus there are 12 ways of checking the correctness of your core quadrant. These 12 checks can help you fill in your quadrant. If you are unable to fill it in, then you could be dealing with either a mask quadrant or a behavioral quadrant (see later in this chapter).

A complete overview of the different options to enter a core quadrant is found in the following diagram.

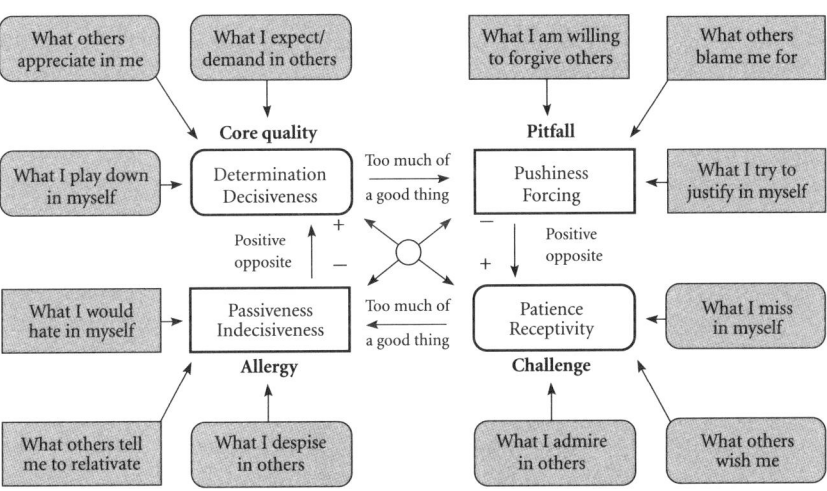

Sometimes things can go wrong when making a core quadrant. The result seems wrong, illogical. Generally this is caused by people mistakenly thinking that the name of the pitfall with the *effect* of the pitfall. The pitfall for dedication would then be described as something like "egotism,"

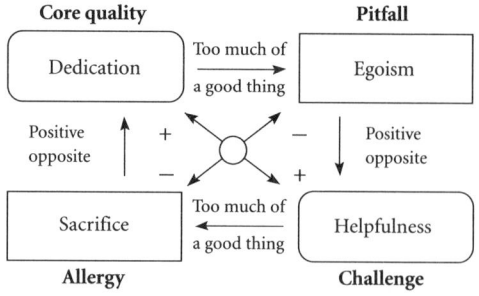

A torsion quadrant

because people see that anybody who is too dedicated (= fanatical) will have the inclination to shut himself off and think of nobody but himself. Egotism is not the pitfall, but result of the pitfall.

The challenge is then described as "helpful" and the allergy just won't fit anymore, or becomes something like "sacrifice," which isn't the right allergy for dedication, because dedicated people are often all too prepared to make sacrifices. In other words, it just doesn't make sense. You could call this a torsion quadrant, because it contains something twisted. Some people find it difficult to distinguish between "the word meaning too much of something" and "the effect of having too much of something" and they have great difficulties with making a quadrant.

The Double Quadrant

Core quadrants are very useful for self-examination. They are also very helpful for managers when preparing for performance reviews with employees. Confronting someone to whom you are allergic can be productive in two ways. By realizing that your allergy could have something to do with your own challenge, you become calmer, more tolerant and your self-knowledge increases. And you can identify the other person's core quality through your own allergy (which is the other's pitfall) by means of a double core quadrant.

Let's say a manager is aggravated by someone he thinks is passive. Precisely because he is allergic to this, he first decides to reflect and determine what this says about himself. He draws a core quadrant of himself on the basis of his allergy, for example the following:

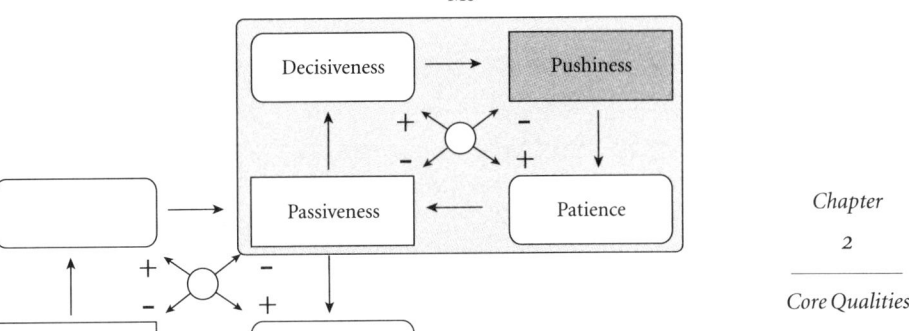

If he recognizes himself distinctly in this quadrant and concludes that it says more about himself than about the other person, this awareness may result in his being less irritated with the person. He has used this incident to get to know himself better and to discover what he still needs to work on in his own development process.

On the other hand, he may decide that, although this quadrant may say something about him, he also wants to discuss the situation with the other person. He will then draw a second core quadrant, assuming that the point he wants discuss is the other person's pitfall. This second quadrant could, of course, simply be a mirror image of his own, which would mean that his own challenge is the other's core quality. But it could just as well be something else, because more than one quadrant can be made for a single quality. These will mainly be differences in nuance, which, however, are just as important.

It is not as if there is some kind of dictionary of core quadrants. The right words have to be found to fit each person: they have to "click," and that means in practice that it is sometimes quite a chore to find the right words. Let us suppose our manager evaluates the other person and develops the quadrant below. Then we would have a double core quadrant.

This double quadrant clearly shows that when the manager loses contact with himself, he runs a sizable risk of becoming "impatient" during the interview and beginning to get pushy. The other person will

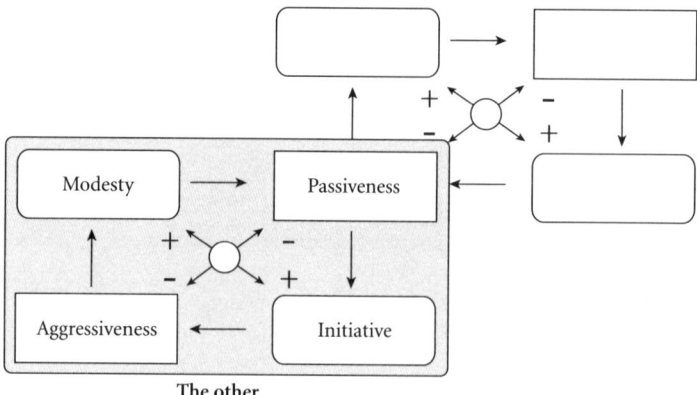

The other

interpret this as "aggressiveness" (his allergy), which activates the other's pitfall and greatly increases the chance that things will get worse and the interview lead nowhere.

Again, it is clear that we have to start with ourselves if we want to (help) change others. This manager can best help his employee by combining decisiveness and patience in himself. If you formulate a core quadrant with an employee, you leave the other "intact." He is not only called to account for what is wrong, but is also told what is right and how he can develop further.

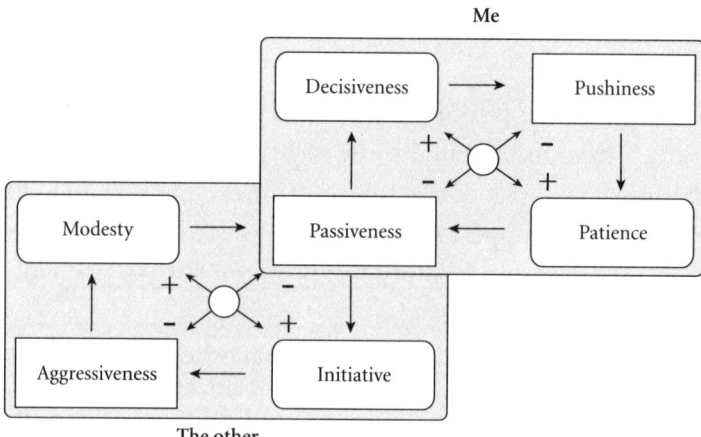

The other

He gets a direction (challenge) on which to work. It makes quite a lot of difference whether the employee is told to be more active or is given the above quadrant. It is surprising how easy it is to discuss people's distortions with them when the whole picture is presented.

John, a 50-year-old manager of a successful department of 60 people, attended one workshop on core qualities. He was satisfied with the way the group supervisors worked. It was just that he had something against one of the group supervisors (Charles). Although he would not want to miss him for the world, he had been irritated for 8 years by the fact that Charles was always so diffident and was, in John's view, not "visible" enough. He wanted Charles to be more expressive, to come across with more conviction. He had hesitated to discuss this with him, because he was afraid of hurting and demotivating Charles, and he valued him too much for that.

Using his irritation with Charles' "invisibility," John made a core quadrant of himself and recognized his own core quality in it, the ability to project himself.

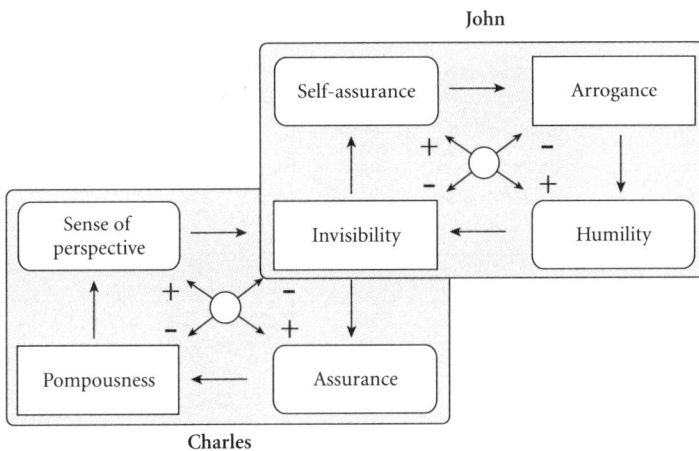

It was wonderful to watch how easily this man projected himself and how he stood up for his opinion. It was also obvious that now and then he tended to go too far and became somewhat arrogant, especially if he felt he was dealing with people he considered spineless. His challenge was to develop some humility. In the core quadrant he made of Charles, he called the latter's sense of perspective one of his core qualities. It was why he valued him so much. Besides, John needed this quality in the department to balance his own assertiveness.

When he had worked out the double quadrant, John discovered how Charles and he complemented each other and decided to discuss this with him. When I ran into him a month later he told me how surprised he had been when Charles thanked him for his openness at the end of their conversation: "At least I know now what you really think of me, what you value in me, and what I can work on for my own development. I also understand much better what you are really like."

Core Qualities under Stress

Core quadrants also reveal how someone tends to react to stress and under pressure. At first, people exhibit too much of a good thing when they are under pressure or stress. In other words they will stumble into their pitfall. If pressure increases, they may, in extreme cases, suddenly start behaving in accordance with their allergy.

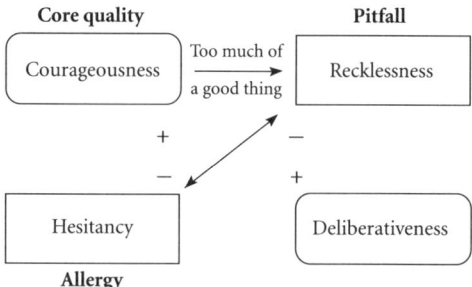

At such times, a person will no longer be recognizable to the people around him, who find his behavior so "unusual" they cannot understand it. Someone who "normally" displays great courage and decisiveness and is considered energetic in his environment, will first become a little too courageous then, under high stress, become hesitant and indecisive.

When this occurs, a "time out" is necessary, or else it may result in a crisis.

The Mask Quadrant

A mask quadrant is a quadrant that superficially resembles a core quadrant, but is actually the exact opposite. A mask is a polished facade intended to produce a certain effect. Masked behavior is characterized by a lack of authenticity. In a way, you could say it is lifeless. Masked behavior is usually taught and maintained by fear, the fear of revealing something you want to keep concealed. The quality a mask quadrant shows as your core quality is not in fact your core quality, but rather a failed attempt to avoid your true pitfall.

On the fourth day of a seminar lasting several days, where managers from various companies were present, the theme was core qualities. In a kind of feedback exercise the participants drew core quadrants of each other and every one was handled in turn. They based their quadrants exclusively on their own experience of the person concerned in the four days of the seminar, since none of them had ever met before. One of the participants was a 54-year-old director in charge of a company employing 500 people. The other participants drew core quadrants representing him as follows:

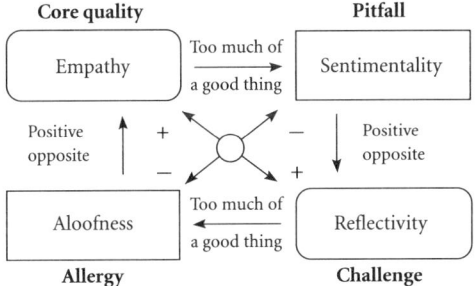

They particularly appreciated his keen interest in other people, and his strong sense of compassion and empathy. They felt that his challenge was to become more rational and reflective. They decided he would be allergic to aloof people. The person concerned reacted with some surprise:

"If you asked my closest associates about this, you would end up with a quadrant the exact opposite of this one. They often say I am very reserved. I think my family would recognize me in this, though."

When he was asked to explain, and tell what he himself recognized most, he answered:

"Inside I am really more like you see me. At work, though, I appear to be different… and I now see why. When I joined the company 30 years ago, my first boss told me after three weeks that I should stop being so sentimental. This was so painful that I decided it would never happen again. From then on, I have behaved in an aloof manner."

This example illustrates how people react to their pitfalls by using their own allergy as a defense. This manager's co-workers would have made a mask quadrant for him that would have been the reverse of his core quadrant. *A mask quadrant is always a (defensive) reaction to an unpleasant experience with an actual pitfall.* The core quality brought out by a core quadrant is the quality to which someone naturally has easy access, such as empathy in the above example. This is not true in case of a mask quadrant, because the core quality it shows is rather this person's challenge.

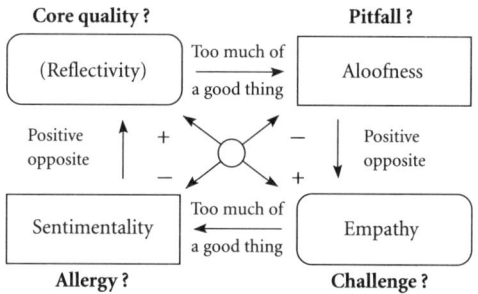

A mask quadrant

If someone tries to avoid his pitfall reactively (because he is against it), he will end up in contact with his allergy. If that happens, there is no chance of growth, only stagnation. The core quality denied, the person concerned becomes "split" and leads a double life. Usually, this results in a crisis or disease sooner or later, after which the person will get another chance to pick up the thread (of personal development).

Mask quadrants can sometimes be recognized because of the fact that they do not touch a chord in the person involved. People are nearly always touched when they look at their core quadrant. It moves them. If not, it may be an indication you are dealing with a mask quadrant, in which case you can consider the reverse quadrant.

Behavioral Quadrants versus Core Quadrants

Some people complete a core quadrant but then can only partly recognize themselves in the results. Generally this leads to remarks something like this: "I may be like that in one situation, but in another situation I react completely differently." If someone says this, then we are actually dealing with a behavioral quadrant and not a core quadrant. A characteristic of a core quadrant is that it exists independently of situations, and therefore cannot be effected by a situation.

When somebody meets another person or observes them, then he is watching behavior. This could, for example, be determined behavior. Behavior is something that somebody externalizes, what he or she shows to the outside world. If you are able to express determination in your behavior, this does not mean it is necessarily one of your core qualities. Or if you express dedication, that doesn't that dedication is one of your core qualities. The question is always whether what you are seeing is the interior or the exterior.

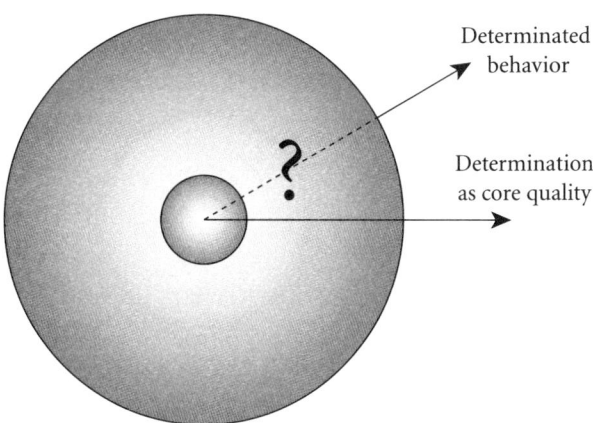

Determinated behavior

Determination as core quality

The problem is that our language allows us to talk about patient behavior and about patience as a quality, and about patience as a core quality. Behavioral training can teach you to adapt and change your behavior. It also helps you to express qualities. This doesn't mean that you have developed a core quality. The mask quadrant that we described earlier is a good example of this. A mask quadrant is a behavioral quadrant and not a core quadrant.

In fact you could say that any quadrant you make of somebody else is by definition a behavioral quadrant, since it is based on what you observe. Of course, I can suspect that this behavior is congruent with somebody's interior. If you listen "from you stomach," you are generally pretty sure, even if you can never be completely sure. And so it follows that I am the only one who is able to make a core quadrant of myself, since I am the only able of looking deep into myself. Often our search for the truth begins by analyzing external behavior. During the analysis, it becomes increasingly obvious what is truly yourself and what has been learned on the way or been encouraged by others. It can also happen that during your trip to the inner you, you start changing the names of the core qualities, the pitfalls, the challenges, and the allergies, that what you originally thought was a challenge can no longer be considered as such, and that you discover that alternative words are better.

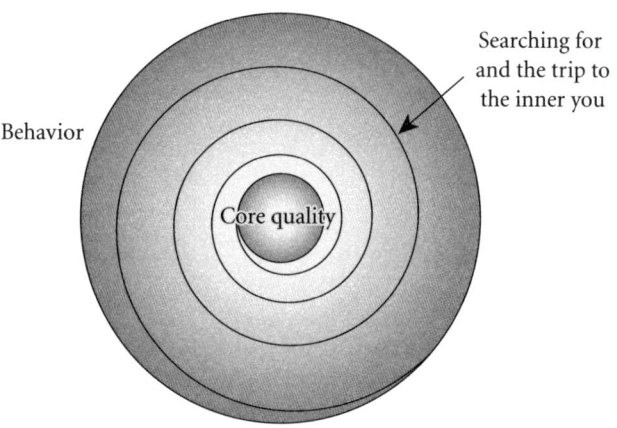

If you discover a mask quadrant of yourself, then it is as if the whole quadrant suddenly flips over and that your challenge is suddenly revealed as you core quality, and your allergy is suddenly revealed as your pitfall. In other words, you can be faced with unexpected surprises. And that makes for some excitement, wouldn't you say?

The Origin of Core Qualities

The question concerning the origin of core qualities is very interesting. Where do they come from and how did they originate? The name core quality already indicates their origin. A core quality originates in the core, which is also called the Self. I assume this core contains not just one or two qualities, but all of them. In their core, people are "whole." There, decisiveness and patience are complementary and not contrary to each other. There, flexible order, lucid empathy and cautious courage are normal. A core quality is, as it were, a gateway to a person's core. It gives (relatively easy) access to it. It is that part of a person still connecting him to his true Self.

The origin of core qualities could be seen as follows. At birth, people come into the world of earthly duality and more or less lose touch with their core. From then on, it is no longer "natural" for qualities such as courage and caution to belong together.

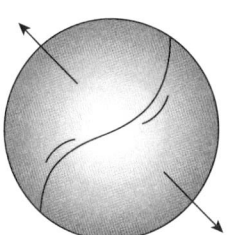 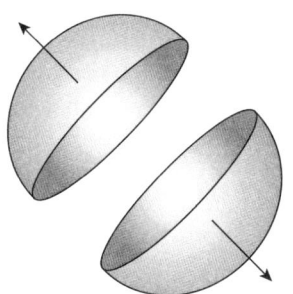

Division at Birth

Since they are no longer integrated, there is a chance that from then on qualities will develop individually and degenerate into too much of a good thing. This can happen to either of both poles. For example, courage can

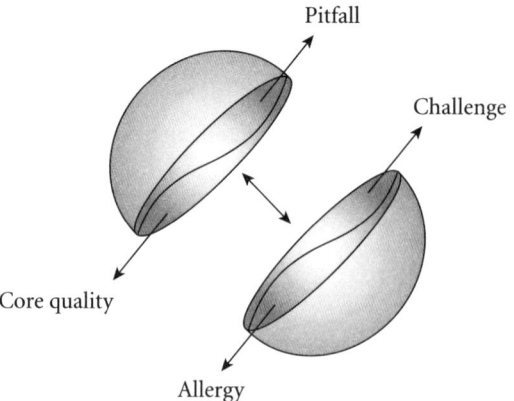

Pitfall

Challenge

Core quality

Allergy

degenerate into recklessness, while caution can turn into cowardice. This is how the four aspects of the core quadrant arise out of the two opposites.

Opinions differ on the reason why one pole later develops into what is now called a core quality, while the other pole becomes a challenge. This difference has to do with one's underlying view of man and the world.

One category of people will ascribe it to childhood circumstances on the assumption that people are formed by their upbringing.

For a second category, the difference is attributable to hereditary factors; they assume that qualities are largely determined by gentics.

A third category will impute it to the Creator, who determines the qualities with which you are born. They assume that qualities are given.

A fourth category believes that man has more than one life and that the soul will always create the circumstances it needs to combine new qualities in its present life to continue growing and to become whole. They believe that people are responsible for the core qualities they have developed and that this is their purpose in this life.

The truth of the matter is not really relevant in this context. In fact, the question remains of whether it is relevant at all. The core quadrant can make a useful contribution to a manager's self-knowledge however he views humanity, although it will determine the assessment of its meaning and value.

The Development Process in a Core Quadrant

It should be clear from the above that people have more than one core quality; in their core they even have them all. People cannot, of course, be reduced to core quadrants, nor are core qualities static. Different core qualities can emerge during every stage of life. In short, healthy people grow (spiritually). Most important in this respect is to achieve a balance. Imagine someone with access to two qualities in the proportion shown below; the larger the size, the better developed and more easily accessible the quality.

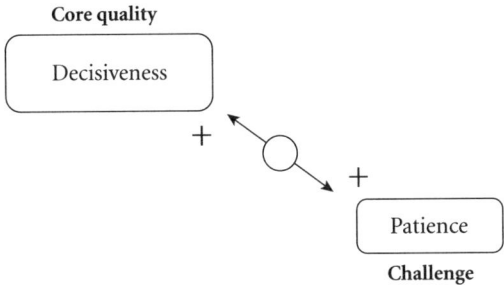

This almost certainly means that in the quadrant as a whole the pitfall and the allergy will be even larger. The allergy will probably be largest of the four, especially if the feeling of disdain is strong. Proportionately, the core quadrant might look as follows:

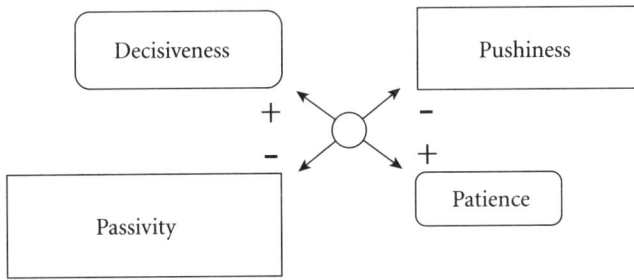

This would suggest that the greater the imbalance between core quality and challenge, the stronger the allergy and the pitfall become. Or in other

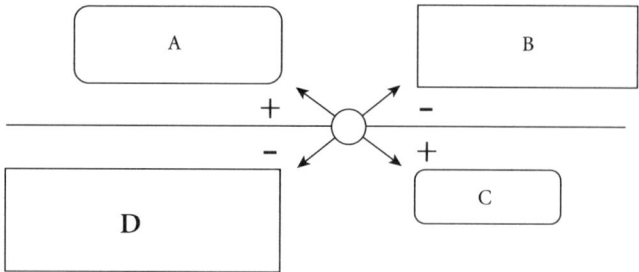

words, the weaker the challenge, the bigger the problems. The calculation for the surface area would probably be: Core Quality (A) + Pitfall (B) = Challenge (C) + Allergy (D).

Now what is the best way to learn how to handle this? There are three paths: *fighting, healing* or *doing nothing*. If you choose to fight, you combat your pitfall. You end up with your allergy, which means that fighting your pitfall is a very ineffective path. You just tell yourself not to be so pushy. But then the only thing you are doing is telling yourself what not to be, and this is very unproductive. You do not change, because you are only trying to be something other than what you are because you wish to avoid something. This way, the energy is directed *against* yourself, which is neither pleasant nor effective. The harder you try not to be something in this way, the more you will stand in the way of your actually changing.

If your goal is change, you will achieve the opposite—stagnation. You will be reactively trying to force something with your will, which is the opposite of creation.

Change is the result of becoming whole by learning to *accept* yourself as you are, including any less attractive qualities. If you choose the path of healing, the most important task will be to learn how to observe; not so much by doing anything, but particularly by inner observation without judging, let alone condemning yourself. To sharpen your capacity for inner perception, it may be useful to go into therapy for a while, provided the goal is to learn to observe. Not every type of therapy is suitable for this. The time has not yet come that managers are valued in their environment for proposing to learn more about themselves (through therapy). Most corporate cultures react fairly allergically to therapy, as if "asking for help" were a sign of weakness.

The way to healing is one of observation, awareness and acceptance of feelings, in that order. Acceptance does not mean resignation—that has nothing to do with self-acceptance. Acceptance refers to your attitude to yourself: you can be *as you are* to become *who* you are. As a result, you will change. Your core quadrant will look different after a while.

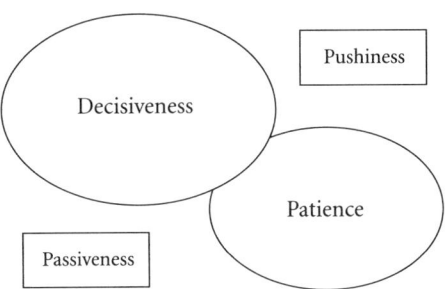

Decisiveness and patience will be more balanced and come closer together; the pitfall and the allergy will shrink and finally dissolve (in the core). Then that part of a person has been healed, and the creative energy originating in the core is accessible.

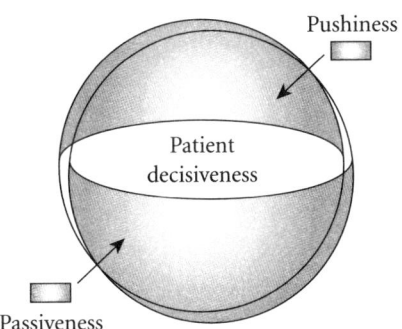

The Energy behind the Distortion

A striking feature of all leadership theories is that they tend to ignore the darker side of human nature. What is this force or energy that drives people into their pitfall, that makes obedience degenerate into servility, and self-assurance into arrogance? We find this energy in the zeal and fanaticism of the activist, the politician, the artist, the evangelist, the lover and the manager.[4] We see it in the businessperson's dreams of expansion and the ambitions of one earnestly pursuing a career. We also find it in a stagnant form in the lassitude and wait-and-see attitude prevalent in some organizations, or in the lower echelons' obedient submission to the higher.

This energy is actually pure creative energy from our core. It alienates us from our core by a process of inner division and imbalance, becoming either a raging river sweeping us along and overwhelming us, or it solidifies and we become rigid. A pushy person has been overwhelmed, while the energy has solidified in a passive person. An inconsistent person allows himself to be flooded, while an inflexible person allows himself to become rigid. In both cases, people are victims of what happens to them (due to their inner imbalance), rather than the creators of their own life. They are guided by their energy instead of guiding the energy themselves and using it to create.

Access to this energy is through the core and through remedying (healing) the imbalance. By becoming aware of his own core qualities and everything connected to them, the manager can nourish contact with his core and restore balance within him, so that his creative energy becomes available for creation.

³] Wishing versus Choosing

> Courage is the willingness to be afraid
> and act anyway.

Wish versus Choice

Confronted with others' successes, people often say: "I would like some of that too…" Then with a sigh, audible or not, they add, "Oh well…"

If a good concept is characterized by simplicity, the concept contained in this chapter certainly meets the criterion. It is all about how to realize a wish, how to be a success at what you really want to do. In other words, how do I create what I want, both as a manager and a private person?

- Why do so many managers have time management problems?
- Why are so many managers stressed out?
- Why do so many quality programs yield so very little and after a while peter out?
- Why do projects take much more time than foreseen, even though they are carefully planned?
- Why do good intentions and resolutions often come to nothing?
- Why does so little come of all the plans we make?
- Why did the free weekend I had so looked forward to just slip through my fingers like sand?
- Why can't I quit smoking?
- Why did all this hard work make me lose touch with my children?

The problem in each of the above examples is not so much one of not wanting enough, but of not *choosing*! It is amazing how many managers allow themselves to be taken in by co-workers and by themselves when they say they want something, or when their co-workers say they want this or that. For some reason, everyone expects it actually to happen. If a general manager asks one of his managers to finish a report and he agrees, there is absolutely no guarantee he will in fact do so. And yet we often leave it at that. Listening carefully to someone who wants something, you can nearly always hear the "if" behind their words.

"I would like some of that myself … *if* I had the resources … *if* I had the manpower … *if* I had the time … *if* my wife would back me up" etc. Since these conditions are hardly or not at all met, it is not hard to predict that this person will come and tell us three weeks later why it did not succeed. It is not that he did not want it enough, but rather that he did not *choose* to actually do it. He probably still wants to do it!

Bringing about changes or results has little to do with "trying." It takes more than good intentions to get results.

The possibility of failure is inherent in trying, and this does not help create the energy needed for the realization process. In other words:

"Wanting" something is the spark that starts the engine; "choosing something from within" is the fuel needed to obtain results.

The secret of success is the ability to make creative choices. Making a choice directs the creative energy towards your goal. You start creating with this energy and become the author of your own life and reality. It is as simple as that!

At the same time, this may be the most difficult task for a human being to perform consistently, because it has far-reaching consequences. Suddenly, I can no longer blame my boss for having to work another weekend, because it is the result of my own choices. I am no longer a victim. The responsibility is put where it belongs, with the individual.

Powerlessness

Failure to achieve something you want is often blamed on external causes, circumstances or someone else. This is like saying: "It is not my fault." It is a way of declaring yourself powerless. Powerlessness is the source of a great deal of (unnecessary) problems in organizations, and lies at the heart of problems of stress, time management and of many sicknesses and lack of vitality.

People do not get sick from hard work, but from lack of purpose and powerlessness.

Powerlessness is often an expression of self-pity. It is destructive, because pity (which is not the same as sympathy) shows *contempt* for inner strength and the ability of people to shape their own lives. This contempt is internalized in powerlessness and it goes to a person's core, undermining inner strength and inner leadership from within. Accepting powerlessness is denying your own core (qualities).

Few things in an organization are as destructive as powerlessness, which makes it essential for every manager to recognize the extent to which he or she is likely to submit to it. Everyone has the tendency to submit to it now and then. So, once again, knowing yourself means knowing your own weaknesses.

Unifying leadership means saying goodbye to the (mistaken) notion of being powerless and realizing you can always take the *initiative* to create a new situation. If this possibility is denied or not recognized, people will go on reacting to others with little result, which will in turn seem to prove that it is indeed impossible to exert any real influence. This, of course, completes the vicious circle. Consequently, people usually blame their inability to fulfill their dreams on others and just continue wishing and dreaming without converting this into an inner choice.

Anybody who says he is powerless has given up his potential for making choices and thus cut off access to his creative powers.

This has not happened to him; he is responsible for it and has the power to change it.

Creative Tension

As I said before, the secret of the creative process lies in making choices. In many organizations this is called commitment—something to which one is committed. Now what happens if someone makes an inner choice? He or she creates *tension*. If I say, "I would like to lose 20 pounds," nothing much will happen. It will be just one wish among many. But if I say: "I choose to weigh 175 pounds in two months time" (I am 195 now), something will happen inside. It will create tension. This tension arises from the discrepancy between what I want and what my present situation actually is. If a manager tells his staff that the new goal is to increase the company's market share, nothing much will happen in that organization. The moment he says: "I have decided that this company's turnover will increase by 20 percent in a year," his direct associates will sense they are dealing with something that deserves to be taken seriously.

Simply knowing what you want does not create tension. Creative tension arises only if the present situated is squarely faced. Two components are necessary to create *creative tension*. The first is knowing what you want, and the second is knowing what you have, the present situation.

Rubberband

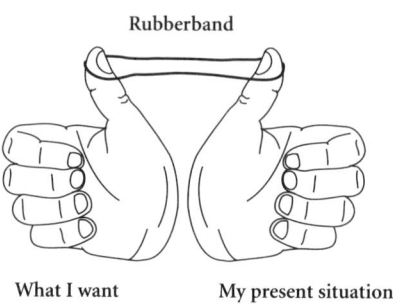

What I want   My present situation

The greater the difference between what you want and your present situation, the farther apart the thumbs will be and the greater the tension exerted on the rubber band. Robert Fritz calls this structural tension and says the following about it:[1]

"Structural tension is not an emotional tension such as fear or stress. Structural tension is a natural tension caused by the discrepancy between the present reality and the desired situation."

This structural tension, which I prefer to call creative tension, is comparable to what happens in a body that has been injured. If I fall and cut my leg, the present reality is that I have a cut leg. The desired reality for the body, however, is for this injury to be closed and healed. The discrepancy between the two situations causes a creative tension, activating the cells of the body to bring about the desired situation (healing).

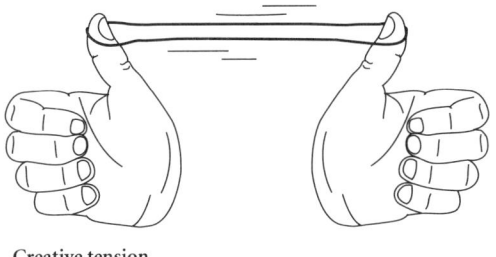

Creative tension

The more creative tension a person can endure, the more he or she can create and realize. A great deal of creative energy was generated in 1961 when President Kennedy announced that he was determined to land a man on the moon and return him safely to the Earth before the decade was out.

Not everyone can endure the same creative tension, and because of this not everyone has the same creative ability. Many people, however, limit their creative abilities by telling themselves:

- "That is too difficult…"
- "That is not realistic…"
- "I really shouldn't do that…"
- "It's really not right…"
- And so on…

Most limitations are self-imposed or imposed by others, not in the least because people consider themselves powerless.

What it boils down to is that you should try to *cultivate* creative tension instead of attempting to reduce it. It is not surprising that so much energy is spent on efforts to reduce tension, because *creative tension* is often confused with *emotional tension,* and the latter is not always pleasant. The difference between the two is mainly that emotional tension results in tensing up, pressure and a sense of obligation, while creative tension gives a sense of relief and "liberation." Creative tension is the result of a creative (healing) choice made from the core, whereas emotional tension is caused by a forced choice made from another part of ourselves (see chapter 4 on subpersonalities).

A lot of tension, including emotional tension, would be created if I chose to buy a five-bedroom house within walking distance of a railroad station, where I could play piano as much as I like and walk around naked in the garden without offending anyone; while my present reality is such that my wife and I live in a two-room apartment in Amsterdam and will need to get a 120 percent mortgage, because we have saved just enough to pay the conveyancing fees. Although the result we want is perfectly clear, the emotional tension still feels rather uncomfortable at times. Consequently, it is normal to have doubts now and then. At such times we have to keep our goal well in mind, check to see if it still coincides with what we want and re-experience the quality of our creative tension, for it is the energy created by this tension that makes us take action.

If we are uncomfortable with our creative tension, we might fall into one of the following three traps:

- We start "nibbling" bits off what we really want, telling ourselves that we have to be realistic and that three bedrooms instead of five is really more than enough. In other words, we start making concessions to what we really want and adjust the result to make it more feasible. In itself there is nothing wrong with this, as long as we are aware that this reduces our creative tension and may accordingly prevent us from realizing what we want/wanted. If this is a conscious choice, we will probably end up with a three-bedroom house and be quite content with it. Although settling for a compromise will relieve the uncomfortable tension, it will also confirm the sense of powerlessness, particularly if it happens often.
- We start denying or distorting and embellishing our present reality, "Our apartment in Amsterdam is really not all that cramped, and actually has three rooms, since the den is also a room … and besides, we are really very happy with the way we live now." This trick will also reduce tension and the chance that we will ever realize what we want. It is just not fair to ourselves. Our present reality may be unsatisfactory, unpleasant or even painful. If we do not start with our actual present reality but with some kind of wishful thinking or illusion, we cannot build up creative tension. You cannot put tension on a rubber

band with only one thumb. We can only build a basis for the future when we are well-acquainted with our present reality.

- We flee into our pitfall or, rather, we let emotional tension chase us into it and start getting pushy, start bargaining very arrogantly, wander around aimlessly (inconsistently) from one realtor to the next, or doggedly stick to our desire for that one house that is so very beautiful but has unfortunately just been sold. In fact, we are abusing our core quality to force a result. By acting in this way, we get farther and farther away from ourselves and our goal. We lose contact with ourselves and our creative power and are finally confronted with the fact that we still do not have what we have always wanted. In this case, tension is neither reduced nor put to creative use. When we fall into our pitfall, an illusion is created that makes it appear or feel as if tension had been reduced, but which in fact produces an adverse effect.

Each of these three mechanisms is reactive. They are directed *against* something, which makes them ineffective in dealing with creative tension. *To create what you want, you have both to face your present reality and have a clear idea of what you want to create.* Your choice for that result causes creative tension, which is converted into creative energy, which in turn mobilizes a power that propels you towards the result you have chosen.

Let me make one thing clear: people do not have to make choices. They are free to cherish their wishes as dreams, with the very real chance they will never be fulfilled. If this is what you choose, fine. I myself have a number of wishes which will probably never be fulfilled—winning a lottery, for example. The important thing is that it does not bother me in the least. If I really want to achieve something, I know I must make a choice. You do not have to make choices, *but if you don't, don't whine about the consequences!*

The process of realizing wishes is divided into six steps:

1 Listening   4 Checking
2 Focusing   5 Choosing
3 Looking   6 Following up

None of these steps can be skipped. If they are, ineffectual choices that do not lead to the desired outcome are an almost guaranteed result.

Step 1 LISTENING

We remarked above that "wanting" something is the spark that starts the engine, and "choosing from within" is the fuel needed to obtain results. This means that it all starts with the first step: What do I really want? You can answer this question by taking the trouble to pause for a while and listen to your "inner voice." Whether it is work or personal relationships, material or immaterial matters, silence will quickly reveal whatever it is you really want.

We not only have to listen actively; it is just as important to hear what our deeper self has to say to us. Often beneath a simple wish lies a deeper desire that you can only hear if your heart is open to it. Wanting something with your mind is different to wanting something with your heart. Creating means connecting your heart and mind and acting from this connection.

For some, the problem is just that they do not know what they want. In such cases, not knowing what you want becomes such a big obstacle that it stifles all other creativity. The only way out is usually simply to invent something, anything. Just so long as you do not get stuck in the "not knowing," because that is something like a plane which will never get off the ground. It is much better simply to take off by inventing something you might want. As things develop, it will become clear whether the wish you started out with is indeed what you really want. If it is not, at least you will have made some progress. In the process you will have learned something about what you do and do not want.

There are plenty of organizations in which personnel (including management) are not encouraged to think about what they really want. Top management does that for the entire organization. "Just do what you are told…" is a common remark. People who really want something are often considered "troublesome." Remarks like "just do what you are supposed to do" encourage people to stay in the background, to wait and to react instead of taking the initiative and coming up with something new. "Who do you think you are…" is another remark that curbs the creative process in its very first stage, as if "wanting something" were egoistical. People give up wanting something to avoid the risk of failure and because they no longer want to feel the resulting disappointment and pain. And yet creation begins with "wanting something," with getting in touch with what you want. This is the first step of the creative process.

During this initial phase, it is important not to restrict yourself to what seems possible or feasible. Wishful thinking is very healthy here, the courage to dream, to fantasize. Their environment does not make this any easier for most people. Every day you can hear comments like, "You've got be realistic," in which realism means "not wanting too much."

By visualizing what you want, you can "discover" what it is that you that you want. By imagining what it would look like, you can discover what you really want. By creating pictures of the future reality and feeling what it is like, you create the connection with your heart.

A courageous list of wishes might be as follows:

- I want time for myself
- I want to enjoy life
- I want to feel fit
- I want to have children
- I want to renovate my home
- I want a nice car
- I want to get rid of these flat feet

The question "What do I want?" is one of the most creative questions you can ask yourself. Not recognizing (or admitting) what you want, simply because it seems impossible to realize, actually means you are denying yourself the truth.

Step 2 FOCUSSING

The second step in the creative process is giving your wishes a clearer focus. It helps to formulate your wish in the form of a result. *Something is a result if you know whether or not you have it.* In a way, formulating the result establishes the position of one thumb.

Result to be realized

If the wish is nothing more than a process, choosing it will not, or only temporarily, generate tension. For example, the choice to work harder will not generate creative tension, nor will the choice to eat less fat. Both are a process, not a result. It is unclear with these kinds of choices when the goal has been reached. If you eat one sandwich a week without any butter on it, you would be eating less fat than if it had had butter on it. And working an extra fifteen minutes once is "working harder." If you cannot put into words what you will achieve, it means you do not know what you want to achieve. Creative tension will not be generated and the chances of success are slight. Emotional tension will become even more perceptible with the imposition of a deadline. Losing ten pounds in two months will generate more emotional tension than losing ten pounds in a year. If the time limit you impose for the realization of your choice is too short, you run the risk of emotional tension overshadowing your creative tension (unnecessary pressure).

The more material in character the wish, the easier it can be formulated as a result. It is more difficult with immaterial or emotional matters. In such cases, it is possible to translate a wish into a result by creating a clear visual image. This is a good idea anyway. For example, wanting to have more fun can be visualized by taking a recurring (work) situation and making an "inner film" about how this would appear as reality; visualize yourself having a conference with a client or at a meeting. How do you sit behind the wheel of your car in the morning? How do you see yourself walking (in this desired reality)? How do you come home in the evening? How do you spend it? And so on. This film can be used to measure your success and can regularly be "shown" in your head to see how much progress you have made.

A more focused list with wishes formulated as results might appear as follows:

- I want one day a week to spend on my hobbies.
- When I go to bed, I want to smile looking back on the day.
- I want to be able to easily run 3 miles.
- I want my wife and I to have a baby together within two years.
- I want to have two bedrooms built in the attic within a year.
- I want a new car with a powerful engine, an automatic transmission and a sunroof.
- I want to strengthen my arches to get rid of the pain in my back.

The better you can visualize a wish, the clearer you will be able to focus your energy. Nearly all successful people do this. They create a clear and conscious image of the desired result and let their actions be directed by this repeatedly confirmed choice. Instead of planning how to go about things in detail, they begin with creating a vivid mental image of the final result. This image works in the subconscious and is manifested as intuition in everyday decisions (which bring you closer to your goal).

By concentrating on the results you want to create first, ways of how to achieve them will develop organically. Asking how before asking what distracts attention from what you want and focuses it on all sorts of problems that may hinder the realization of your wishes. "How can I do this?" Prematurely focusing on the realization process limits effectiveness and creative capacity.

Wanting to be too perfect and thinking your wish has to be fully crystallized before it can be chosen is another problem that can crop up in this phase. What matters is taking a step (towards your choice), see what happens, make adjustments when necessary and then take the next step. Just as all jets flying from Amsterdam to New York are not exactly on course 99 percent of the time, but still reach their destination (because they adjust their course), so everyone can achieve results without being perfect. That is, if they can cultivate the creative tension that arises when you not only have a clear picture of the desired outcome, but also of your *present reality.*

Step 3 *LOOKING (& FEELING)*

This step is about looking at your present reality and is at least as important as determining what you want. It actually consists of three elements: Looking, Seeing and Feeling. When we discussed the development of core qualities, we argued that change should not be a goal, but rather regarded as the result of an inner *healing process.* The same goes here. *Perception, awareness* and *feeling* are essential steps to clarify present reality.

Perception means observing the present reality. What does it look like? What is the present situation? What do I think of it?

By becoming aware you connect this reality with your Self. In other words: In what way am I part of this and what is my role in it all? How did I contribute to winding up in this situation? These usually unconscious contributions (for instance an unconscious choice in the past) have put you in this situation. It can be painful to (have to) face up to that.

The third element is *feeling* what this means and what the consequences are. If you accept your feelings concerning the present reality, it will be assimilated into your core. You will be in touch with the present reality instead of rejecting it as undesirable or fighting it. If you do not accept your feelings, any choice you make will be reactive, since it will not be made from your core. It is important to remember that feeling is not the same as resignation! Feeling means accepting your feelings and facing the plain truth, including your own part in shaping the present reality!

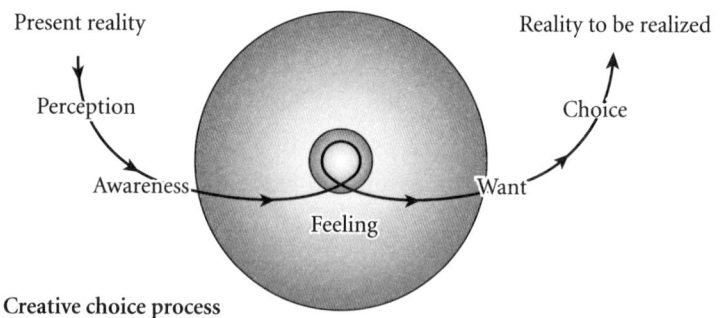

Creative choice process

The choice process entails more than this, however. Perception, awareness and feeling will generate a wish *from inside* you, which will spark creative choices. The creative tension generated in this process could also be called healing tension. That is why creative tension feels so different than emotional tension. When you create something, you heal something. It is an almost irresistible energy that makes it crystal clear what choice you should make. In a way, the choice becomes nearly inevitable.

That is why it is so important to examine carefully the present reality. If this reality should cause dissatisfaction, as it often does, there is a good chance your wish does not come from within you, but from outside, purely in reaction to the present situation. If that is the case, the energy is directed at fighting the dissatisfaction, which means it is *against* something (reactive) instead of *for* something (creative). The goal is to avoid something (dissatisfaction) rather than to create something. There is something you do *not* want. You have skipped the stage of accepting your feelings, and therefore "missed" the core (the source of energy).

If you do not want to face the truth, you will want to create a different reality as soon as possible and escape by making a "choice." The energy for making this choice a success, however, is also external. If I want to find another job because I do not get along with my boss, my relationship with my boss is the cause of my dissatisfaction. As soon as there are some positive changes, I will lose the energy to find a new job, since it was generated by my dissatisfaction. My energy has diminished along with my dissatisfaction. In other words, if you derive energy from something you

Present reality · Reality to be realized

Perception · Core · Choice

Awareness · Want

Reactive choice process

are against, you make the realization of your wishes *dependent* on others. No wonder this seldom results in something you really want, since you have never been in touch with it and consequently it remains hidden. This does not mean dissatisfaction should never occasion change. It very often does. The problem is that reactive choices do not work (are ineffective) if you deny the truth about your own part in creating the current situation and your feelings about it. Reactive choices give rise to counter-reactions, and the "creative process" becomes one long struggle with disappointments and setbacks. This is more of a *reactive* process than a *creative* process.

Determining the present reality establishes the position of the other thumb and gives you a feeling of the emotional tension that will be generated by a possible choice. This emotional tension is often an obstacle to experiencing creative tension. In this phase of the process, creative tension can, as it were, be tested.

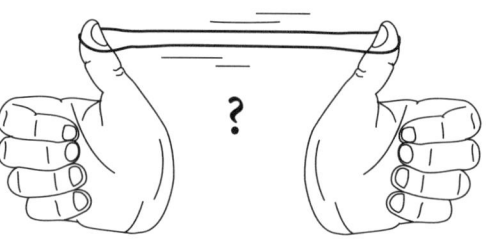

Testing creative tension

As previously said, the difference between emotional tension and creative tension is mainly that emotional tension leads to tensing up, pressure and a sense of obligation, while creative tension leads to relief and "liberation," as if a burden has been lifted (the die is cast).

Relating the present reality to our list of wishes might yield the following:

- I like writing, I am good at tennis, and I enjoy singing and playing keyboard and guitar. The reality is that I do not write, no longer get any exercise and have not touched my guitar for eight months.

- I am quickly irritated and impatient, my mind wanders when I am at a meeting, and I am always judging my co-workers.
- I gained seventeen pounds during the last few years. I started jogging three times. I drink coffee all day, and feel weak and guilty about my lifestyle.
- I have wanted children for years. I don't mention it anymore, because I feel like I am nagging. I am nearly forty. My relationship with my wife is fine; we love each other very much. She still does not want any children.
- We do not really need any rooms in the attic, but it would be nice to have a little more space. I am handy around the house, but I just do not have the time.
- I drive a five-year-old car, which may last another year. Actually I think it is a waste to put money into a car.
- My arches have collapsed, and I do not really believe anything can be done about it.

These are some aspects of the present reality that give plenty of cause for reactive choices. That is why the next step deals with examining the effectiveness of possible choices.

Step 4 CHECKING

Before making a choice it is advisable to check its effectiveness. Ineffective choices are those that generate a new reality that do not bring about what you really want, and as such they are unsatisfactory and disappointing.

Six checks can be carried out that increase the chance of effective choices. They are:

- A check for reactivity
- A check for contribution
- A check for embedment
- A check for conditionality
- A check for action power
- A check for consequences

You have already performed the most important effectiveness check for *reactivity,* about which quite a lot has been said. Is it a choice for or against something? What do I create with it, instead of avoiding or fighting something with it?

The second check is: "What does the result *contribute*?" This can be a contribution to the larger whole of which I am a part, such as the organization I work for, my family, society, etc. If it does not contribute anything, chances are that your environment will be far from thrilled by the idea, and counterforces may arise in your environment to try to prevent its realization. This does not mean you have to change your mind—although it probably does mean an increase in emotional tension—because in the present reality you are the only one who wants it. The greater the contribution of my wishes to the larger whole, the more external support I can expect, which will in turn reduce emotional tension. This is not to suggest "adaptive behavior." People following their inner voice will sometimes go against the current, not because they are being contrary, but because they have something to contribute. If you know what you want and make yourself available as an "instrument," the creative tension (caused by your choice) will allow you to realize the "impossible." We find, particularly if we look at the creation of great works of art in the past, that the contribution was at the time seldom noticed and that true renewal was often achieved *despite* the environment.

I believe the greatest contribution anyone's creative power can make is in healing. As far as I am concerned, healing choices are the most effective. "What needs to be healed?" is the question Steven Levine continually poses in his impressive book *Meetings at the Edge.*[2]

Some of the choices I have made in my life were solely for my own benefit; at least that is what I thought at first. They did not make any noticeable contribution to others. But the simple fact that I made them for myself and by so doing gave myself a present was a healing factor in my own process. For example, everyone in my environment was opposed to my wanting to ride a motorcycle. Yet realizing this wish had a healing effect, in the sense that I freed myself from what others thought was good for me.

The third check is a check on *embedment*. Obviously, not all choices are on the same level. In his book *The Path of Least Resistance*, Robert Fritz distinguishes between *fundamental* choices, *primary* choices and secondary or *supportive* choices.

A fundamental choice is one that concerns your entire life and your attitude towards life. A primary choice concerns concrete results; it is a more or less complete whole. Writing this book is an example of this. Supportive choices are those that support a primary choice, for example my buying a laptop to write this book. The more a choice is embedded in a higher-level choice, the more effective it is. In a certain sense, all supportive choices confirm primary and, one hopes, fundamental choices. A few examples of fundamental choices:

- I choose to be the determining creative force in my life.
- I choose to give meaning to my life.
- I choose to be healthy.

If you are confronted with contradictory wishes or choices inside yourself, it means you have not (yet) made a choice on a more fundamental level. If you are torn between choosing for your career or your family, a fundamental choice is needed. This problem cannot be solved at the level it occurs. A solution to this inner conflict can only be found at a higher level. If you choose to give up smoking (primary choice), this will be a lot easier if it is embedded in the fundamental choice to be healthy. If you have made this choice, you will do or not do certain other things as well, since a fundamental choice concerns your whole life and will probably not be limited to smoking or not smoking.

The fourth check is a check for *conditionality*. The question is what conditions, if any, are attached to possible choices. "I choose to complete this job today, if my secretary makes sure I can work without being disturbed…" This is not a choice, but still a wish. Everything may go according to plan that day, but then again it may not. It does not depend on the manager, but on the secretary. Conditional choices greatly undermine creative power.

Say I chose to buy a new house within three months on the condition that I get a 120 percent mortgage. One day I come across the house of my dreams and I go to the bank. I sit down and an assistant in the mortgage department starts explaining the bank's rules.

"You need 120 percent? That's going to be a problem. You know, we don't normally offer more than 70 percent of the value upon fore-closure...' and so on and so forth.

"Well, it may be a little difficult, but I really do want that house and I am sure I can pay the mortgage."

"I understand that Mr. Ofman, but those are the rules ... Why don't you start with something smaller and return in a few years?"

"Yes, well, I guess there's little else to do. But, anyway, I am going to try somewhere else first ..."

Now here is a different situation.

"You need 120 percent? That's going to be a problem. You know, we don't normally offer more than 70 percent of the value upon fore-closure..." and so on and so forth.

"I understand that perfectly (I knew that when I faced the present reality), and I know rules are rules. I have come not so much to ask for something as to offer you something. I am offering to let you finance my house. Over the next 30 years, you will be able to make a lot of money on me. Are you interested?"

"Well, let's see..."

Some people will call this a bluff or an assertive sales technique, which is exactly what it is if it does not come from within and is used as a trick. Then it will not work. If someone deliberately walks into a bank to get what they want in this way, they will probably be disappointed. If a person has made an unconditional choice and as a result of this walks into a bank to arrange financing, they will be open and alert and unwilling to force things. They do not have to. Their contact with their goal will often allow them to find ways to reach it.

The fifth check for effectiveness is *action power*. If a choice involves another person, you move outside your own direct area of responsibility and power for this action and make yourself dependent on others' willingness to change. For example: "I choose for my boss to be open to my ideas." In a way, this is a conditional choice. The action is not my responsibility and therefore outside my ability to take action. I am only responsible for the action of creating something myself. I could say: "I choose to work in an environment in which people are open to my ideas."

The last check is for *consequences*. It may seem unnecessary to ask yourself: "If I could have it, would I take it?" Yet some people would be unpleasantly shocked if their wish were suddenly fulfilled. And since the chance is great it will be (if this person has made a choice), it is a very good idea to make sure he or she would really be happy with it.

This means imagining the final result. Sometimes people gain new insights and discover that the consequences of the final result are not really what they want. If you choose to occupy a certain management position within 5 years, it is perfectly possible that that is exactly what you will be doing, although the loneliness of your new position may not be quite what you expected. The consequences of having a baby is that you have to change dirty diapers and cannot go to the movies whenever you feel like it.

Step 5 CHOOSING
The first phase of the creative process is not finished unless a choice for a result has been made. That is the moment you make contact with yourself—and experience the creative tension in you. Physically feel it.

The moment you say, "I choose to (have created)…" you take a step out of your reactive Self into your creative Self, as it were. At that moment, tension is created and energy mobilized. It is the *turning point* from victim to master, from reacting to initiating, from impotence to power. In terms of energy, it makes a big difference whether someone says, "I want to be healthy…" or "I choose to be healthy…!" The former statement does not generate energy, while the latter does. "Wanting" incorporates the possibility of failure due to some (external) reason; "choosing" something means accepting full responsibility for achieving the result. In doing this, you stick your neck out, recognizing that achieving the final result is up to you. This is the moment when people are most directly confronted with their own doubts. It takes courage to make choices.

Step 6 FOLLOWING UP

Once the choice is made, it is important to continue to follow what happens. If you have made an inner choice, "doing" things will seem almost effortless. Sometimes you may "catch" yourself doing something to bring the result a step closer. If things are as they should be, action will be somehow *self-evident* and almost effortless. The creative tension will ensure that you stay alert to signals from the environment. Sometimes, the way something can be achieved only becomes clear *after* you have made a choice. Apparently, it takes tension to find the right way.

For example, the person with the flat feet had no idea what to do about it. Only after he had made the choice for healthy feet within six months did he "happen" to meet someone who turned out to be a "footologist." Once you start making choices you will possibly find that things do not just "happen." Sure, it happens to you, but you have definitely played a part in it.

When a group supervisor of an insurance firm chose to be group supervisor of another department within six months, he was dumbfounded when his manager asked him to assume that position a week later (coincidence?). People find that coincidence happens just a little too often to be called coincidence. That's why it's not about following, but about "being." Be amazed, be alert, be open, be happy and be thankful for what you receive.

As soon as your actions become somewhat forced, it is time to reconsider what your inner wishes are and what choices you have based on them. Forced actions are a sign of lack of trust in yourself and your own creative force, an expression of emotional instead of creative tension. As soon as emotional tension creeps in, people try to force the result and almost certainly fall into their pitfall… etc.

It should be clear that everyone can adjust their choices at all times.

That too may take courage sometimes, because some choices have or can have far-reaching consequences for the rest of one's (working) life. Consider, choices for a life partner or a new job or a second career. However, you are never bound to a choice once you have made it. *You can always make another choice.* People who no longer see this as an option, render themselves powerless and a victim of events.

Dealing with Setbacks

"Yes, but there are always a few things you cannot do anything about, which simply happen to you…," some people will say.

Obviously, no one is omnipotent. It is true that, if you lose your job because the company for which you work goes bankrupt, this is something that just happens to you. It does not make you powerless, though. It is possible to make new choices in every situation. You may choose to accept the situation, or you may choose to take action against it. Every new reality, however painful, offers an opportunity to make new choices. Acceptance is not at all the same as resignation. Acceptance means facing the truth, "This is the new reality…" The truth is naked, clear and sometimes painful. Accepting a new situation becomes a lot easier if it makes sense to you. To be able to see the sense of something, one has first to *give it meaning*. Giving meaning to something is a creative act that releases energy or keeps it flowing. One can always choose to give meaning to an event, however painful it may be. *The choice to give meaning to something is a fundamental choice (for me).*

Events you experience as meaningless (read: those to which you do not give meaning) are difficult to accept; they usually lead to resignation, which is something completely different. The main difference between acceptance and resignation is that acceptance releases energy (you release it), while resignation blocks (obstructs) energy.

Choosing to accept a situation is not always a matter of turning a switch, though a conscious choice can speed up the process of acceptance. Coming to terms with emotions takes time. Elizabeth Kübler Ross[3] distinguishes a number of natural phases in the process people go through to come to terms with their emotions.

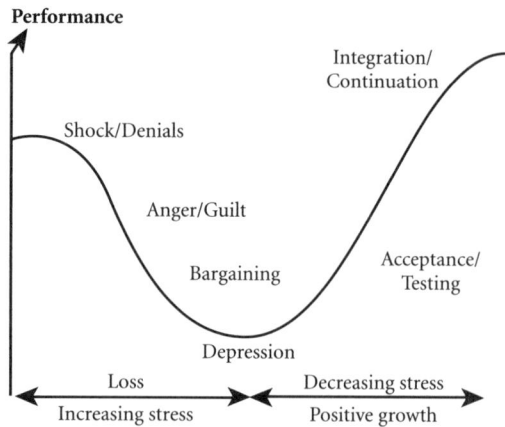

The process of coming to terms with emotions

Phase 1 *SHOCK AND DENIAL*

This is the phase of initial shock and disbelief, often expressed as denial. People refuse to believe that what has happened is real and has actually happened. Reactions such as "No it can't be true, there must be some mistake," are fairly standard. By simply pretending nothing has changed and/or by gritting their teeth and carrying on, people try to play down the meaning and consequences of what has happened. This phase does not usually last long and depends on whether the change was unexpected or not, and whether it was self-initiated or forced. In this phase it is useful to perform "down to earth" tasks, to structure your day, make a list of priorities determining what should be done first and what last, and give things time to get sorted out. It does not help to pretend nothing has happened and to refuse to talk about the situation. Some people get hung up in this kind of behavior, hoping it will turn out that the change never happened.

Phase 2 *ANGER AND GUILT*

The main emotion in this phase is anger or rage, which may be directed outward (towards someone else) and can take the form of reproaches, punishment and attempts to blame someone else. These expressions of emotion are usually attended by a sense of impotence. The anger can also be directed inward (towards oneself), expressing itself in self-reproach, guilt and feelings of frustration: "If only I had…" In this phase, it really sinks in that something is going on, which may also cause fear. It is well-known in dismissal procedures that, after an initial phase of silence and lack of reaction, people display a frenzy of activity in their work, re-investing energy in all kinds of activities and showing a great deal of commitment, while investing nothing in finding an alternative. It is important in this phase for people to determine for themselves if and when they need support and that someone stays in touch with them, so that they know someone is there for them whenever they want to talk or need support, anytime they choose.

Phase 3 BARGAINING

The third phase is the bargaining phase, in which people try to reach a compromise in order to maintain as much of the old situation as possible, and attempt to minimize the perceived negative consequences of the new reality. This usually means trying to escape the new reality or denying it.

As yet, there is no energy for examining new possibilities. The time has come to face how this situation really affects people. The time for emotions has come. People often start smoking, eating and drinking more during this phase and neglect their health.

Phase 4 DEPRESSION (THE PIT)

In this phase people are really down in the dumps. It is preceded and accompanied by feelings of failure, loneliness and even despair. The energy level is low, as are motivation and self-confidence. This is the phase almost everyone tries to escape, trying with all their might to avoid the feelings that accompany it, while admitting these feelings is exactly the point. Fighting them nearly always turns out to be much more painful than experiencing them. The only thing to fear is fear of suffering itself. By admitting and experiencing these feelings of disappointment, pain and sadness, people are healed. At that moment, true acceptance begins and inner growth becomes possible. "Having to do things" or "well-intention-ed advice" is not the point. In this phase, isolation is very common, and it is essential to pay attention to this and avoid making blunders. It helps if people are encouraged to express themselves, to admit their feelings of impotence and depression and are not left alone with their feelings.

Out of fear for these kinds of feelings, people may relapse into an earlier phase and start "circling:" first they are angry with others, then they blame themselves, then again they try bargaining etc. If that happens, a clear confrontation may help this person to overcome his or her resistance.

Phase 5 EXPLORATION OF NEW POSSIBILITIES

In this phase, people let go of the past and start exploring new limits and possibilities. People tend to work on the new possibilities with great (sometimes even excessive) enthusiasm and look forward into the future rather than back into the past. A great deal of new energy and vitality has been released, although people relapse into earlier phases once in a while. It is an exciting and often tiring adventure to find the right balance between investment in the future and letting go of the past by reflecting and discovering new limits. For many people, it also helps to experience a clear moment when the past is over and done with and the new situation begins.

Phase 6 INTEGRATION AND CONTINUATION

In this phase you discover new meaning in life and integrate this into your everyday routine. Life takes its course again. Hopefully, there is time to enjoy the new situation and the lull and calm of integration before a new change occurs. This phase usually starts with inward contemplation following the enthusiastic outward exploration of new possibilities. The question sometimes comes up of what it was all about, and what the deeper significance of what happened was. In this phase, people often feel a need to support others who are going through the process they recently went through. In the latter stages of this phase, all attention is focused on one's own life and work and the new situation no longer takes center stage. Integration is complete, and it's on to the next change.

This process demonstrates that people are not simply robots who can have complete control over their lives simply by making choices. It will be clear that some people pass through these phases more quickly than others, and that the process of change does not follow a linear course. In practice, we go back and forth, from anger to letting go, from deep depression to great enthusiasm for new opportunities, from clamming up like an oyster to acting like a screeching baboon. This is not to say, however, that people cannot create a new reality in every situation by making creative choices.

Making a choice sets the creative ball rolling. Many things will happen during this process. The present reality will undergo continual change; unforeseen events may cause people to reconsider whether they still want what they thought they wanted. Every day, they will make or be able to make dozens of choices that bring the final result closer.

No one says it will be easy to make choices like this. Again, it takes courage to live and work this way, but what you get in return certainly makes it worth it. Taking your life into your own hands and knowing that, whatever happens, you can always create a new reality, can cause tremendous feelings of satisfaction and self-respect. You no longer feel like a victim of circumstances or events, but alive and actively influencing what is going on instead of being lived by others. Making inner choices makes people come alive and renders organizations vital and healthy. People take responsibility for their own lives and start making contributions to the organizations they belong to, be it their company, society or family. Man's creative force is much greater than many people have dared to hope. It is about time we started using it.

How does a manager create an organization in which the people he supervises take responsibility for their own (professional) lives, behave like parts of a larger whole, act on the basis of their core qualities and fulfill their wishes? That remains the issue. Part of the answer has been dealt with here: by choosing to be part of an organization in which people learn to make their own choices. The essence of unifying leadership is *helping people (learn) to make their own choices!*

4] Who Actually Chooses?

The waves of the sea inside
Are like the rising and falling tide
And on the surf froths and churns
The question that forever burns
Who are you…?

The Will

A great deal has been said so far about wishing and very little about the will. What about it, what is its function? Will-power enables people to express themselves; it is the means of self-expression that gives the core or "I" its voice. Its function is to *channel energy* and direct it;[1] it is a fire-hose in the hands of a fireman. Will-power enables the "I" to *direct and control* energy, it enables the core to manifest itself in the different core qualities.

Without will-power, people are like leaves carried along by the wind of fortune, at the mercy of anything they may encounter: events, experiences and all sorts of thoughts and feelings. People without a will are rare, although you do find people who rarely use their will. They are like fire-hoses thrashing about on a lawn. There are also people who use their will without being aware of it. In that case it is not clear who is holding the hose.

In our society, will-power is easily associated with pushy, exacting, forceful or authoritarian behavior, all of which are distortions of excellent qualities, as if the will's function were only to pursue one's own interests and get one's own way. This often happens if people start using their will as a way out of their pitfall, but that is not what the will is for, that gives it negative connotations. Will-power is apparently considered a threat. People unconsciously sense that this is something with potential, exerting a great deal of power. They are right, because the fire-hose can be a source of both good and bad, depending on who wields it and what his or her intentions are. During the past centuries, the church in particular saw to it that the will was bridled and focused on higher goals. As a result of our

The Will?

increasing awareness and the shifting paradigm, it looks as if the time has come for people to accept responsibility and discover their will. People beginning to make conscious choices will discover and experience the force of their will; they will experience that their will is their implement to give direction to their energy and vitality.

Who actually Chooses

In the previous chapters, I have repeatedly argued against making reactive choices, and in favor of making sure that you choose from the center, the core, the "I." How do you know your choice comes from the "self" and is not some distortion or pitfall? "Assagioli's egg"[2] is a useful tool for discovery.

"Assagioli's egg" is a kind of map of the inner self. First of all there is the *lower subconscious* (1), which is the part of our subconscious where all our memories, experiences and the past events of our lives are stored, as well as the repressed experiences that lie dormant somewhere deep down. The *middle subconscious* (2) "houses" those experiences and aspects that we can become aware of when we choose to. This leads them to the *field of consciousness* (4), the part of our personality that we are consciously aware of.

The higher unconscious or *superconscious* (3) comprises everything that is still in store for us, our as yet unrealized potential. This where our inspiration and intuition flows from.

79

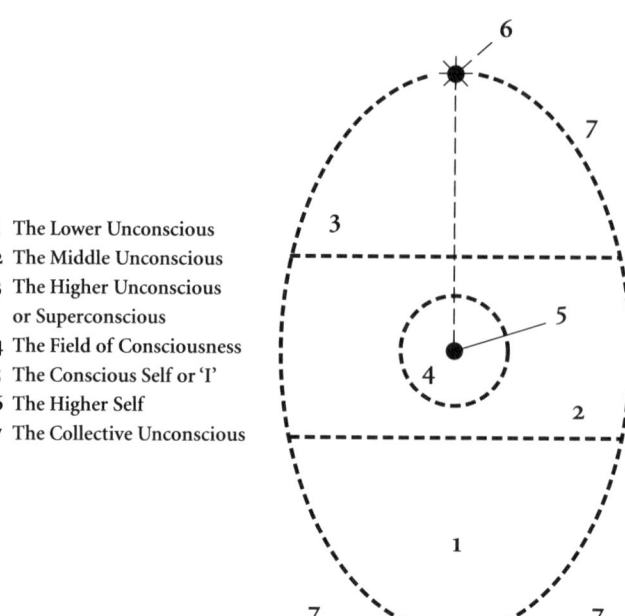

1 The Lower Unconscious
2 The Middle Unconscious
3 The Higher Unconscious
   or Superconscious
4 The Field of Consciousness
5 The Conscious Self or 'I'
6 The Higher Self
7 The Collective Unconscious

Speaking in terms of time, the lower subconscious deals primarily with the past, the middle subconscious with the present and the super-conscious with the future. The dotted line surrounding the personality indicates that people are linked by the *collective unconscious* (7) and there-by influence each other. People are not isolated entities, but drops in an ocean (collective unconscious).[3]

Occupying the central position is our conscious self, or the "I" (5), which is the center of our consciousness, the part where we experience ourselves. The "I" can perceive and direct our entire personality, can focus the will and make choices. It gives us a sense of identity. It is the basis upon which we develop our challenge and achieve balance when our core quality is imbalanced. The "I" is the never-changing point inside that always remains the same. Becoming aware of this center leads to union, healing and acceptance. The transpersonal or higher self (6) is also ultimately experienced through the conscious self. The "I" can also be regarded as a reflection of the higher self, or as "its projection in the field of consciousness."[4] Healing choices are choices made from the "I" in connection with and inspired by the higher self.

In computer terms, the lower subconscience is the back-up discs or tapes in my desk drawer, which hold all my data. The middle subconscious can be compared to the hard disc of my computer, from which data, including viruses, can be retrieved at all times. The field of consciousness is my working memory, the information I am currently working with. The superconscious is the as yet unrealized potential present in my laptop, which I know nothing about and do not make use of. The collective unconscious is my modem connection with various data banks and networks. I am the "I" operating the cursor or mouse and making the choices.

When making choices, the important question is how to ensure you are in touch with this "I." If people take time to think about themselves and listen to their inner voice, they will find they have several "I's," as it were, also called *subpersonalities.*

Subpersonalities

A subpersonality is a part of us that has become independent and has started acting as a separate personality. You may discover a part which might, for instance, be called the judge, or the saboteur, the teacher, the careerist, the gourmet, the hippie, or the little boy. Within our personality, these subpersonalities lead their own lives, each with their own habits, thoughts and feelings. They are sometimes recognizable as inner voices.

Assagioli paints the picture of our personality as a bus with the "I" as driver and the subpersonalities as passengers. When taking a curve or approaching a crossing, a subpersonality will sometimes come up to the driver and call out: "Stop…!" at which the hippie will say: "Cool man… put the pedal to the metal!" In short, the gathered subpersonalities in the bus do not always agree or want to go the same way. If it all ended with a subpersonality shouting or demanding something now and then, it would not be so bad. Problems start when the subpersonality pushes aside the driver, takes over the wheel and starts making his or her own choices.

If that happens, the choices made are nearly always reactive and therefore ineffective. Subpersonalities tend to react "reactively," because they themselves often originated as reactions to some experience. They are crystallized experiences from which conclusions have been drawn. Subpersonalities tend to seek confirmation of their conclusions and even

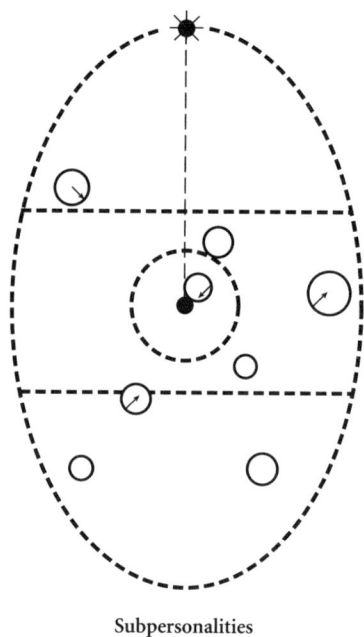

Subpersonalities

to create confirmation if they get the chance. The "victim" subpersonality, for example, may very well have come into being when the person in question got into a situation in which he or she felt completely powerless. Particularly if this is a recurring experience, the conclusion drawn may well be that "there is nothing you can do about it anyway…" That conclusion begins to lead a life of its own and may have a strong influence on the life of a person in the form of a subpersonality, which will regularly call out from the back of the bus that "making choices is useless, because the others won't cooperate…" and so on. This makes it rather difficult at times to make choices, because before you know it, it is not the "I," but some subpersonality that chooses.

If a careful choice has been made and it still proves impossible to stay in touch with the result, it is often a subpersonality which is not really interested in that choice. It may be very useful to determine afterwards that you were being sabotaged by a subconscious part of the self, but it would have been even more useful to have had this out in the open in advance. One way of doing this is to identify the undermining sub-personalities.

Let's say someone wants two hours a day free in which to work without interruption. Before choosing, he seeks out the part in himself that sits snickering to himself in a little corner, rubbing his hands together, saying: "Well, we'll just have to see about that, won't we… look at him, it's all bluff…I know it doesn't work that way, because… just wait and see, you'll find out that… my time will come… heh, heh, heh!"

By "giving voice" to such a part or subpersonality, useful information is provided about potentially undermining forces (unconsciously) present in this person. Listening to this information and paying attention is exactly what brings out that part into the conscious mind. Putting the subpersonality in the spotlight, as it were.

Then it is very important how you treat such a subpersonality. The worst thing you can do is try to throw it out of the bus. That is impossible, it would mean repressing it or sending it back to the subconscious, which is exactly the place where it can do most damage. The problem is not that the subpersonality exists, but that the "I" is unaware of its existence. That is when a subpersonality can slip into the driver's seat unexpectedly when no one is looking. In other words, a subpersonality that is not given any room and is not accepted, gains even more influence.

The same applies here as was true for core qualities and choices: first perception and awareness, then feeling and wishing and, finally, choosing. The most important one of these is feeling. Accepting the subpersonality's feelings means the "I" makes room for it and is prepared to listen, for subpersonalities always have something meaningful to say, they represent something. What it is exactly they represent can be discovered by making one or more core quadrants for this subpersonality, in order to discover the core qualities underlying the distortions.

The question remains how the "I" can be distinguished from a subpersonality. By gaining more insight into the different subpersonalities, it becomes clear that these are always moving and changing. They are triggered and driven by external influences. Yet there is something inside that does not depend on external influences, something that can perceive without immediately reacting, the central "I" with which we can become aware of our various subpersonalities and perceive them. The "I" is the center of consciousness, it is recognizable by its lack of *obligation and pressure*, and it always has a number of options. The feeling that goes with it is one of *space, freedom, chances* and *opportunity.* Subpersonalities always are and feel restricted; they are all about what you have to do, ought to do, and are allowed to do.

When I decided to get my motorcycle license a few years ago, it never occurred to me that I might fail. A few minutes before the test I noticed I was driving in an unusually tense manner. When I (rightfully) failed my test and saw all my beautiful plans go down the drain, I tried to find a subpersonality that might not have agreed with my choice to get my license. I soon discovered there was a passenger on "my bus" with clear ideas about taking tests:

"I will no longer take tests! Who does the jerk in the car behind me (the examiner) think he is anyway? I am my own boss, I have my own business and no one tells me whether I am good enough or not. I will be the one to decide that! Get out of my face!" I could not say I was pleased to discover such arrogance in myself, but it was the truth. Right before I had to take the test a second time, I took a minute to pay some attention to this bus passenger. I invited him to ride along with me and told him that, this time, I was the in charge. The tension was gone and I really enjoyed riding during this successful test.

In my opinion, the main contribution of the concept of subpersonalities is that it helps us to disassociate ourselves from the parts we often identify with. I am a victim becomes "part of me feels a victim," immediately creating more space. I am a manager; I am number one; I am a chicken; I am a wimp; I am an artist, etc. These are all examples of identification with one aspect of the self. Plenty of people end up believing that this is what they are. They sell themselves short, because the "I" is much bigger than all these parts.

In abridged form, Assagioli's disassociation exercise goes as follows:

"I have a body … but I am not my body …"
"I have feelings … but I am not my feelings …"
"I have desires … but I am not my desires …"
"I have thoughts … but I am not my thoughts …"
"I am myself … a center of pure consciousness …"

Learning to see our inner selves as subpersonalities can help us to see ourselves as a whole Self, and thus to discover the center of creative energy from which we can make creative choices.

Make a Deal with Yourself

People who make clear promises and keep them are usually respected. Reliability is highly appreciated in others. Why not be reliable to ourselves? Why not keep the deals we make with ourselves as we do with others? A choice is a deal you make with yourself. I promise my boss I will have the minutes of the meeting on his desk by four o'clock tomorrow. I make a deal with myself not to drink any alcohol tonight. By making choices I reach agreements with myself. Carrying out these agreements gives me self-respect and more self-appreciation.

Thus making choices leads to more self-respect. For the subpersonality lacking self-respect, this is a bit of a shock. It is quite possible that this subpersonality, this bus passenger saying "I am no good anyway," dislikes the whole idea of making choices.

Why?
Because he came to that conclusion years ago.
What does he think of making choices?
Well, nonsense of course,… it doesn't get you anywhere!
What did "I" do with all this?
I listened to him and decided to keep my word anyway.
Why do I keep my promises to myself?
Because "I" want to.
Why do I want to?
Because that way, I achieve what I want.
Is that necessary?
No, it isn't, but it happens anyway.
What's it good for?
Hang on a second…, what are you really after…?!
Oh… you just wanted to check if I were really "I," really my Self.
Satisfied…?

Power or Omnipotence

Creator or co-creator? As we have already said, making inner choices releases energy and directs it towards a desired result. This energy gives you a feeling of power, and the greatest danger in that is the feeling of *omnipotence*. People are capable of the most incredible things. Research has been done, for example, into "spontaneously" cured cancer patients, people who had been given up by medical science and yet were cured somehow. They tried to find the common denominator in all these cases, and it was found that all "victims" had reached a stage in their disease when they took matters into their own hands and no longer let others tell them what to do. They began making their own choices, sometimes to the dismay of the people around them, because suddenly they seemed less sociable. The therapies they underwent were different, but the results were the same.

Another study[5] revealed that rats that cannot exert influence on their environment are much more likely to get cancer when injected with cancer cells than rats that can. The first group's immune system was clearly less capable of fighting the foreign cells. It has also been physiologically demonstrated that the degree to which people can influence their environment, or at least think they can, affects their health.

We should not conclude from the above that, if only people would make creative choices, they would not get cancer, or worse, that someone who has cancer has only himself to blame for living such a reactive life. This is a fallacy and absolute nonsense.

The important thing is to start using the incredible potential inside of ourselves and to create organizations that encourage people to do so, organizations that are vital and healthy and in which people can creatively realize their potential.

Part Two

The Creative Organization

Power is just the ability to act
…
If the ability to act is not focused
with a sense of purpose
or a sense of spirit
or a sense of service,
then it will eliminate life
STEWART EMERY

5] The Developing Organization

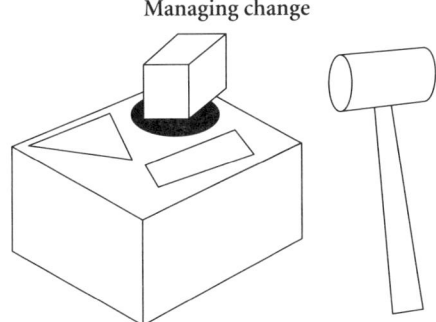

Managing change

A bigger hammer does not help!

Free Energy

In Part One, we discussed the individual creative process. Hopefully, it has become clear that an individual does not have to be a victim of his or her environment, although that does not alter the fact that his/her environment influences an individual. In some organizations, the principles we described will be easier to put into practice than in others.

Questions we will be dealing with now are:

- What are the characteristics of a creative organization?
- What development process must an organization go through to become one?

"There they go again, I wonder what the top has thought up now...!" or other such complaints are often heard at the start of yet another program. I know a number of organizations that go through one program after another, like some kind of ritual, programs with impressive names like Total Quality Management, Strength through Cooperation, Get it Right the First Time, Decisive and Customer-Oriented Action etc. A substantial amount of time is invested in kick-off meetings, workshops, seminars, task forces and coordination meetings, while the majority of those present ask themselves where to find the time to tackle even more projects.

Most management consultancies have some kind of phased plan for organizational change. One has 4 phases, another 12, but what they all have in common is their top-down structure, with "active" participation from top management, which tries to control and "stay on top" of the whole process. In my opinion, this is intended to keep the illusion intact that they really know what the result will be. If you look at the practical results, the only possible conclusion is that most change processes produce disappointingly few results.

The reason this is so can be found in the consciousness with which these processes are implemented and managed. If top-down meant "from the mind downwards," it would not be such a bad approach. Most programs are reactive, however, and aim to fight or avoid something, to avoid complaints, for instance. Since people are not creating something, enthusiasm for this kind of program usually diminishes rapidly.

As far as I am concerned, developing organizations is first and foremost about locating the available *"free energy."* Whether it is a total quality program, the introduction of a "project approach" as a way of structuring the work or a computerization process, the right approach depends on who really wants what in an organization and why. What gets people going, what appeals to them, what makes them *enthusiastic*? Taking advantage of "free energy" is usually the best approach to get a development process rolling. This is a *process of searching* for answers. There is no one best way, no phased plan to guarantee success. Development, as opposed to envelopment, means uncovering, peeling off one layer after another. What will be revealed under these layers cannot be predicted with 100 percent certainty. One usually has an idea of what the next step might be, but it will have to be confirmed by reality.

Alignment & Attunement

The role of leader in development processes entails ensuring *alignment* and *attunement*,[1] or in Roger Harrison's words:

"Alignment occurs when organization members act as parts of an integrated whole, each finding the opportunity to express his or her true purpose through the organization's purpose…

"With Attunement we mean a resonance or harmony among the parts of the system, and between the parts and the whole. As the concept of alignment speaks to us of will, so that of attunement summons up the mysterious operations of love in organizations: the sense of empathy, understanding, caring, nurturance, and mutual support."

There is a power in words. When we call the love we find in our organizations by other names than its own, it loses its power. I suspect we are reluctant to name love because to do so will release that power, and we do not have forms and processes with which to channel it. We do speak, somewhat gingerly, about caring, open communication, consideration, and the like. But not about love.

When we do think about love and organizations, we are apt to see love as a *disruptive* force, destructive of order and good business judgment. Images come to mind of managers making personnel decisions on the basis of affinity and friendship, or setting prices based on the needs of the customer. Of course, people do sometimes make business decisions by consulting their hearts, but it is seldom admitted, and there are certainly no business school courses on how to do it.

Successful organizations, inspired by a higher goal, also display the drawbacks of this "inspiration:" obsession. The families of managers and employees often pay the price for this obsession, and eventually managers themselves are affected by it too, asking themselves during their mid-life crisis why they are doing it anyway. Feelings of guilt about what they have done to their families, however, often cause them to drown themselves in their work again, so they won't have to feel the pain. This "socio-environmental pollution" is rarely considered destructive, however, but rather encouraged and stimulated by the organization as an expression of commitment and dedication. Alignment and Attunement also means that families are looked at as integrated parts of the whole, and not separated from it.

Directing Energy

Most managers are allergic for chaos. If they understood that chaos is the existence of energy without direction, then perhaps they would be a little less allergic and instead direct their energy at directing the energy within the organization. But how can you do that?

The word "energy" is being used more and more in management world. "There's not much energy in this group…" or "that costs a lot of energy" are expressions you hear almost daily. Everybody seems to know what these mean. It is quite remarkable how many energy terms from physics have found their way into our daily vocabulary. We talk about power, tension, resistance, friction, load, current, force, capacity, pressure, transformation, strength etc. All these terms have something to do with energy.

We are gradually learning that everything is energy and that even matter—as Einstein once said—can be considered a "dance of energy." It is obvious that energy plays an important role in organizations. Yet "management of energy" has meant relatively little over the years, although I believe that management world will discuss it a lot in the coming decades.

What does "management of energy" mean for managers? How do you release the energy in an organization? How do you get energy to stream through the organization? How do you direct energy? What is energy, anyway?

Let us start with that last question. The dictionary calls energy the force with which something is done or aimed at. The "force with which" suggests that energy is colored by qualities such as perspicacity, resilience, simplicity, caring, determination and so on. And thus a variety of energies are the result: perspicacious or caring energy, ordering, irritating, determined or applied energy etc. Thus qualities color energy, and this gives energy many guises and allows energy to be experienced in any number of ways. In terms of energy, you could say there were two kinds—creative and reactive energy. Creative or creating energy can be found on the positive axis of the core quadrants; reactive energies are found on the negative axis. A characteristic of creative energy is—as we have already mentioned—that it is for something, rather than reactive energy, which is always against something.

If you were to set out a core quadrant on a horizontal axis, then it would look something like this:

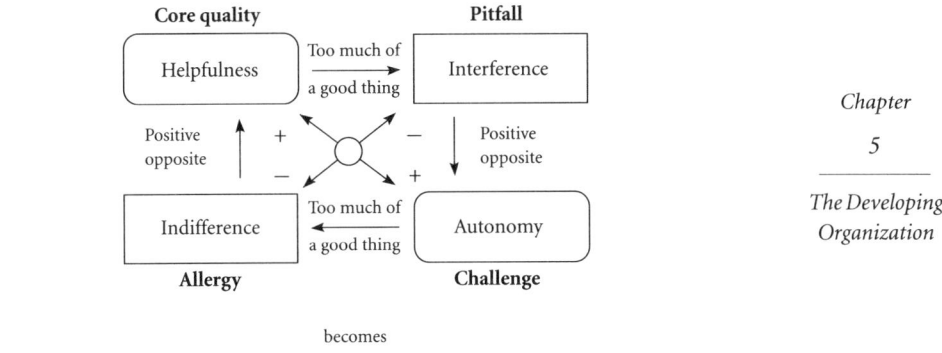

In this way, it is even clearer that core qualities arise from the core or the source (they are not called core qualities for nothing!) and that their disguise is the result of a loss of contact with the source. When a person knows his or her core qualities, tunes into them, and reveals them in his or her actions, then that person is making contact with his or her source, his or her core. Energy that comes from the source is always positively charged, creative, and creating. Only when the energy is too far removed from the core does it receive a negative charge, becomes reactive, and becomes counter-productive. In other words, creative energy stimulates life, while reactive energy leads of "death." Both are parts of the reality in which we live. Energy can thus receive a positive or negative charge. This charging of energy can be done consciously—once we have become conscious of the possibility! You can use your Will to make choices that are positively charged. The possibility of creative energy devaluating into reactive energy will all depend on the degree of balance or imbalance we have. If determined energy is balanced with patience, then it can be used creatively. If there is an imbalance in the direction of determination, then the chance is that it can turn into insistence.

If we accept that every person has a number of core qualities, and therefore a number of core quadrants, then the energy field is determined by the sum of each person's dominant quadrants. An energy field could be seen as the area of influence, the reaction of the energy source, the working area of somebody's core. Just as ripples on a lake spread out from a single stone, so does the influence of a (human) energy field spread through an organization. There is one difference however: unlike the ripples in a lake, the influence of the energy field remains long after the stone has sunk from sight.

Everything that exists has an energy field, whether that is created by a human being, or by nature (of which man is also a part). If it is a human creation, then we can recognize the energy color of the qualities or their distortions of their creator and experience them in the work. This is true of art, music, architecture, but also of a memo, somebody's office, or the feeling in a conference room where a disagreement has just occurred. The same is true of this book.

As far as energy sources are concerned, I am assuming that everything that appears to be an external energy source is in fact nothing more than a stimulus that creates a connection to a person's own source of energy. This is important, since it implies that there is no other source of energy than the inner source of an individual, the core from which he or she creates.

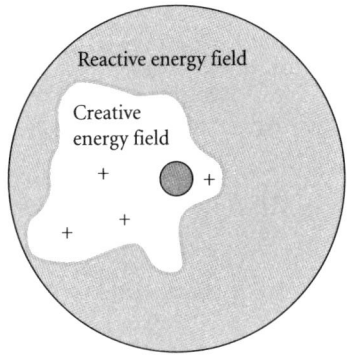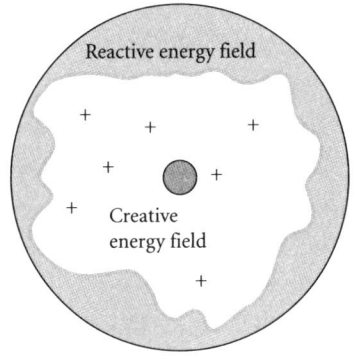

Energy fiels of two different persons or organizations

This means that an organizational aim cannot be a source of energy, nor can the values of a company be a source of energy, and nor can any compensation be a source of energy. In my opinion, these are actually energy fields that can be either stimulating or repulsive, depending on whether they have a predominantly creative or reactive character. But they are certainly not sources of energy. At most they are stimuli that can encourage people, but they have irrevocably a temporary character. This doesn't detract from the fact that it can be pleasant to work in a stimulating environment. When I was writing this book, I constantly sought out places that helped me get closer to my inner self so that I could wrote from that core. Generally these places were abroad, in mountains, in nature, by the sea and always alone. For me there is only one source of energy: my inner core. That this core is fed by something greater than myself is for me a given. But how it works remains a mystery to me.

Although—thank goodness!—man is rather more complicated than a single core quadrant, his energy field is generally generated by relatively few dominant core quadrants. These could be four or five different quadrants, or they could also be a number in the same "category." One way of visualizing this energy field is a "quadrant circle" in which the most important core quadrants are set out as lines. Let us say that we are dealing with six core quadrants; in that case, the quadrant circle would look something like this (see page 96).

This says nothing about the degree of balance or imbalance. In order to make this visible, we must divide each energy field into a creative and reactive part.

A positive energy field arises from the positive axes of the core quadrant (core qualities and challenges). The pitfalls and the allergies result in a reactive energy field. Both energy fields share the same core or source. There are no sources of negative energy. The energy field mentioned earlier (using six core quadrants) could be expanded further, in which case it would look like this.

A quadrant circle is something like an energy scan. Using it, you can determine which core qualities (energy colors) are already present and work towards the realization of the aim, and which still need to be developed.

It is important when depicting energy in this way that the total of creative and reactive energy remains the same. In other words, energy

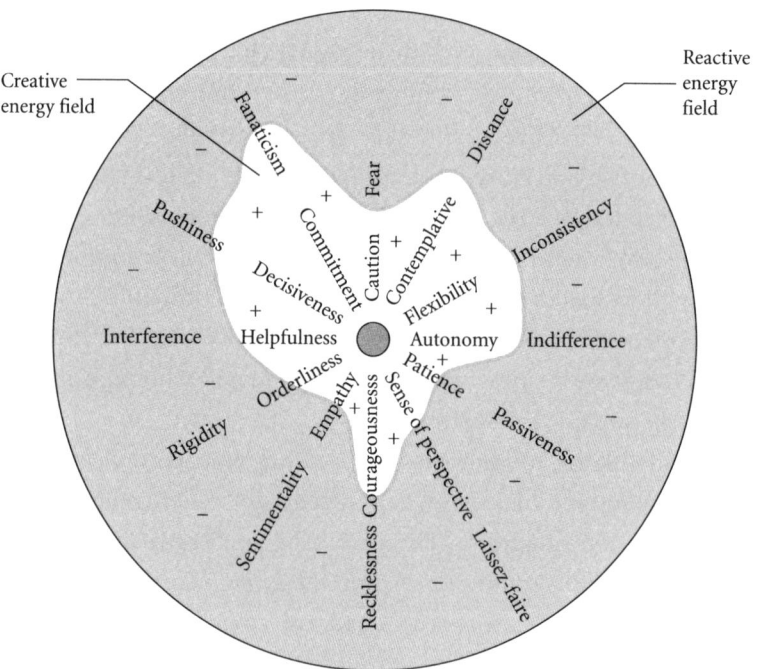

Quadrant circle from an energy field of 6 core quadrants

cannot be lost. It can be used reactively (= ineffectively), but creative energy is always present. The question is: what should we do with it, how should we direct it. For directing energy, there are, I believe, three positions:

1 Mobilizing and directing human energy within organizations is the primary responsibility of a manager.
2 Mobilizing and directing an organization's energy is the key to change.
3 Energy follows nature's path of least resistance, wherever that may lead.

An organizational structure is a system of canals through which energy flows—both the energy of the organization as a whole and the energy of each individual working in that organization. Blockages in channels results in a lack of creative energy in one place and an excess of reactive energy in another where other outlets—not contributing to channeling the energy towards the goal—are sought.

Linda Ackerman once wrote: You could think of an energy channel as a river or canal through which energy flows. If everything is right, then all the energy will flow towards the final goal: the end of the river or the canal. But if a channel is blocked, or a channel is dug in the wrong direction, then the energy flow is impeded. And so you can ask the following questions about the channels:

- Which channels are necessary to achieve the goal? What has to happen strategically and practically to achieve this goal? (Think about authority and consultation structures, communication networks, production processes, sales channels, advisory bodies etc.)
- Which channels already exist? And in which of these channels can blockages that have either built up spontaneously or been thrown up by people be removed or can the direction of the flow be changed?

The leader can ensure first that the organization stimulates the flow of energy and second that the energy is routed into those channels that help the organization achieve its aims.

If we accept this vision, then it will be necessary to develop a new style of leadership that can support the new generation of leaders in their present deliberations about complex situations and change. This leadership style in which the leader is expected to ensure that the organization not only has structures and procedures, but also has the energy to achieve the aim could be called "bundling leadership." The essence of bundling leadership is to help people be creative in making choices. By turning wishes into creative and effective choices, the Will is activated and energy is released and directed at the organization's aim.

Inroads into Development Processes

As we have said before, the first thing to do is locate the available free energy. The question is, what is best suited to the organizational culture? There are different approaches: the "It" approach, the "We" approach and the "I" approach.

The *"It"* approach is the most impersonal; approaching things from the "It" side means working on *"It:"* system, procedures, regulations, structures and primary work processes.

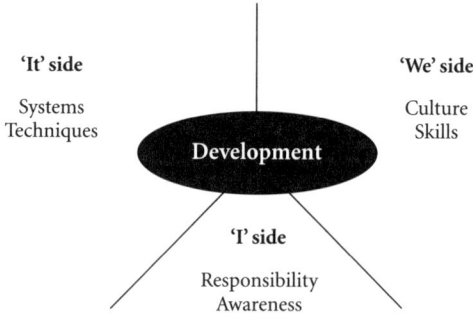

The basic principle of this approach is "measurement is knowledge"; decisions are based on facts rather than on opinions. If someone says "That is something that always goes wrong here," the first question will be,

"How often is always, what is that and where is here?" This is the domain of management *techniques*, or tools. Systems are analyzed and optimized by logical, rational and linear thinking. Most organizations first ask for more tools, more techniques, more knowledge. This can be a good approach to the development process, provided the other dimensions are dealt with in subsequent phases. Quality programs, particularly those of the 80s, focused primarily on an organization's "It" side. The enormous interest in the project approach is caused by the wish to achieve results by means of a different way of working. As one top manager once said, providing more and more tools results in an escalation of intellectual violence comparable to the arms race.

Starting on an organization's *"We"* side means working on its cooperative climate, its *culture,* teamwork and identity. It means paying attention to what unites people. Good systems and procedures work only if people can and will work with them. If the organizational climate is such, that, given half the chance, people will try to pull the rug out from under each other, improved systems or tools will only be used to fight each other even harder. Problems are not infrequently caused by corporate culture—that complex of deep-rooted habits—rather than by structures or systems. Insight into how cultures work is a prerequisite for every manager who must be able to manage development processes. The "We" approach entails the development of interpersonal *skills* to create an open atmosphere in which creativity can flourish. Analyses of cause and effect and Pareto diagrams are only of very limited use in this respect. As the problems are of a different nature, it takes a different approach to solve them.

The *"I"* approach emphasizes personal initiative and the individual *will* and *responsibility* to make choices and act creatively instead of reactively. This requires inspired and enthusiastic leadership, based upon self-knowledge and insight into personal core qualities. The ultimate objective is for every individual in an organization to make his or her own choices, choices that are based upon alignment and attunement. The "I" side could also be called the inside of the development process. It is not about techniques or skills, but about *developing consciousness.*

This (tripod) model can be particularly useful in the earlier stages of a development process, to discover where it is best to begin. In a "go-getter" culture, it will probably be best to start with the "It" approach. In environments that are free of external threats, the culture approach (see next chapter) often works very well, while the "I" approach can be very suitable for environments that are rife with tension and "sore points."

There is no such thing as a phased plan for development processes. As we said before, developing an organization is a trial-and-error process, in which, ideally, the management is just one step ahead. Sometimes, they must conform to expectations as much as possible, at other times, it may be advisable to do something completely unexpected. This mostly depends on what management wants and *chooses*.

The system approach has been largely left out of this book. The following chapter deals primarily with the culture approach to development: how to create a structure and a culture that results in a creative organization, and what characterizes such an organization.

6] Organizational Culture

Culture

That something like organizational or corporate culture exists is hardly new. The importance of organizational culture has been widely recognized. That is why it is so strange that corporate culture is still such a cloudy and intangible concept. This chapter discusses a number of ways to lend more substance to the concept of organizational culture.

In many ways, the impression is created and enhanced (by literature on organization theory, for instance) that there are logical and rational solutions to organizational problems, particularly to those concerning the structure of an organization (the "It" approach). We often find, however, that conflicts arise concerning the way organizations are organized; chosen structures are implemented with difficulty and have to be changed after a while. The cause of these problems, which engender a great deal of tension, is often the failure to realize that those who have an interest in an organization (management, employees, third parties) perceive the organization and its problems in different ways. What people perceive depends on their own values and norms: their ideas about how people should behave with each other, why they must cooperate, their views of what society should be, etc. These values and norms are the basis of people's choices concerning the organization, i.e. how it should act, how it should be organized (objectives, structure, processes, technology). Taken together, the individuals' norms and values and the choices based on these form what one might call *organizational culture.*

When we talk about organizational culture, or corporate culture, we mean the whole network of codes of behavior, or, as they say, a company's countless *written and unwritten rules* dictating expected, encouraged and rewarded behavior. When people deviate from this behavior, corporate culture determines what they will be called to account for. These codes of behavior can best be pin-pointed by looking for signals people give each other, such as, *"That's the way things are done around here!"* This makes it clear that one must observe these habits and cannot deviate from them without impunity. The following statement is a simple example of culture, "We have a really enterprising culture here. That is something that is typically expected and encouraged here, something you will be called to account for if you deviate from it."

Culture has to do with behavior that has become "normal:" *habitual* behavior, *ingrained* habits. It is important to gain insight into these habits, because an organization is an organism that functions like the human body. If something is implanted that goes against the habits of that body, *rejection mechanisms* are triggered. If new ideas or methods are introduced into an organization, they also trigger rejection mechanisms. If these could be revealed beforehand, they could be anticipated. This is true for all processes of change, for example the implementation of a new computer system or a quality program.

Harrison's Culture Diagram

Roger Harrison wrote an inspiring article on different cultures,[1] in which he describes the four main variants:

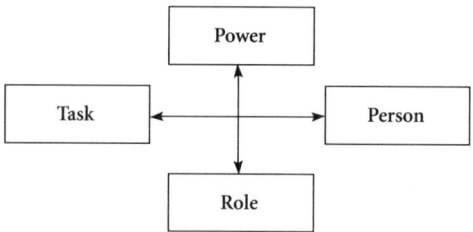

Each of these is described in further detail below.[2] We assume these cultures are "pure," although in reality they very rarely are, with intermediate forms being usual. The examples used have been taken from Charles Handy.[3]

POWER CULTURE

A spider's web can serve as a symbol of this. These cultures depend on a central power source, with influence spreading from the central figure. There are few rules and procedures. Control is exercised by delegating power to key figures and placing them in vital positions. Within the organization, managers fight for every personal gain they can get, even at the expense of their colleagues: the law of the jungle prevails.

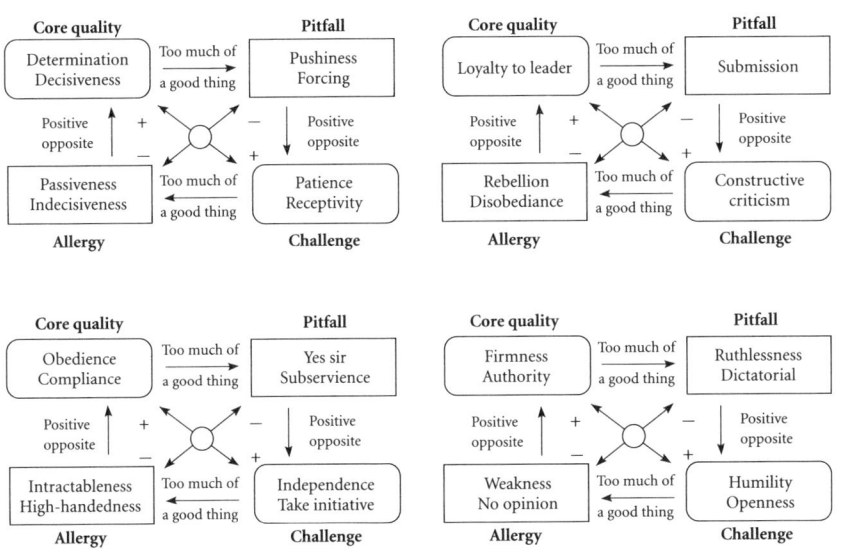

Core quadrants of the power oriented culture

A power-oriented organization will attempt to dominate its environment and eliminate all competition. The organization itself does not want to be subjected to any kind of power or law and will often try to increase its control over its environment, at the expense of weaker organizations. Such organizations are ruthless and will sometimes even resort to illegal means. In a power-oriented culture, "Quality of Service" means praising the customer to the skies so that he will indeed almost think he is "always right." Such organizations probably distinguish between different classes of customers and treat them accordingly.

ROLE CULTURE

Role culture is often stereotyped as "bureaucracy" and can be symbolized by a Greek temple. The strength of a role-oriented organization are the pillars, the functions and specialisms coordinated at the top. The pillars' work and the relations between them are dominated by a large number of rules and procedures; people fulfill precisely defined roles.

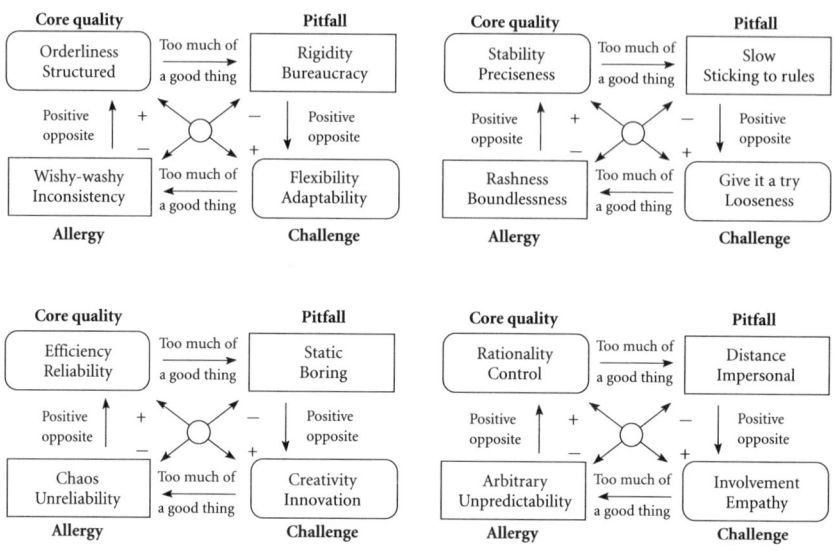

Core quadrants of the role oriented culture

Role-oriented organizations strive to achieve the greatest possible degree of order. The position of individuals and organization components within the larger whole must be clearly specified. Decisions concerning these positions must be based on objective arguments. Responsibilities are clearly defined. Nobody steps outside of their specific field of responsibility. In role-oriented organizations, behavior is very predictable; correct behavior tends to be appreciated more than effective behavior. Stability is as important as skill. The procedures for changing organizational policy and structure are roundabout. The organization, therefore, is incapable of adapting adequately to changes. "Greek temples are insecure when the ground shakes!"

The first thing a role-oriented culture will associate with "Quality of Service" is setting up customer-service systems as efficiently as possible, that operate cost-consciously and quickly.

Note: Role orientation often develops as a reaction to power orientation. An attempt is made to control infighting with various rules, procedures and mutual agreements about task responsibility.

TASK CULTURE

Task-oriented cultures strive to achieve a higher aim, which may be making profit, winning a war or reorganizing a department. The most important characteristic of such organizations is that their structure and activities are judged solely according to the contribution they make to this (higher) aim. Nothing must stand in the way of achieving this goal. If rules and procedures slow down decision-making, they are changed. If individuals lack the skills or technical know-how to perform a task, they are retrained or replaced. If personal needs threaten to reduce the effectiveness and speed with which decisions are made, they are suppressed. Authority based only on power and one's place in the organization is not considered legitimate. Authority should be based on know-how and skill.

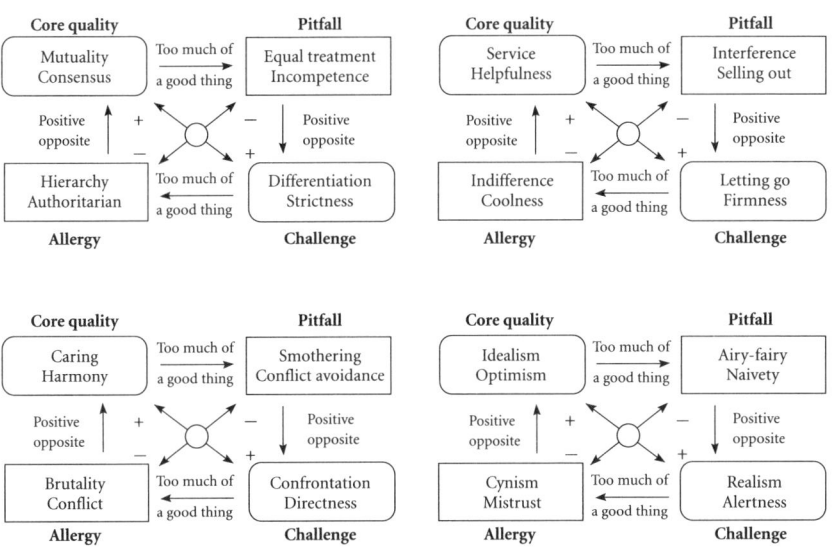

Core quadrants of the support oriented culture

105

The general attitude is very pragmatic. The corresponding structure can best be portrayed as a network or matrix. Where "Quality of Service" is concerned, people in a task-oriented culture will first of all think of what they can *do* to positively influence the customer and have him cooperate. The relation to the customer is one-sidedly determined.

PERSON CULTURE

Contrary to the previous three types, the Person-oriented organization primarily serves the needs of the individuals (people) within it. The organization enables its members to fulfill needs they cannot satisfy anywhere else. This is the basis upon which the members evaluate the organization; if it no longer enables them to do as they please, it loses its reason for existing. That is why person-oriented organizations are usually short-lived. Leadership tasks are rare in these organizations. If it is absolutely necessary, someone will be given a managerial task, the choice being made on the basis of ability. Members are expected to influence each other, for example by being attentive and helpful and setting a good example. Preferably, decisions are made by consensus. Unpleasant tasks are shared. The past few years, there has been a noticeable trend towards a more person-

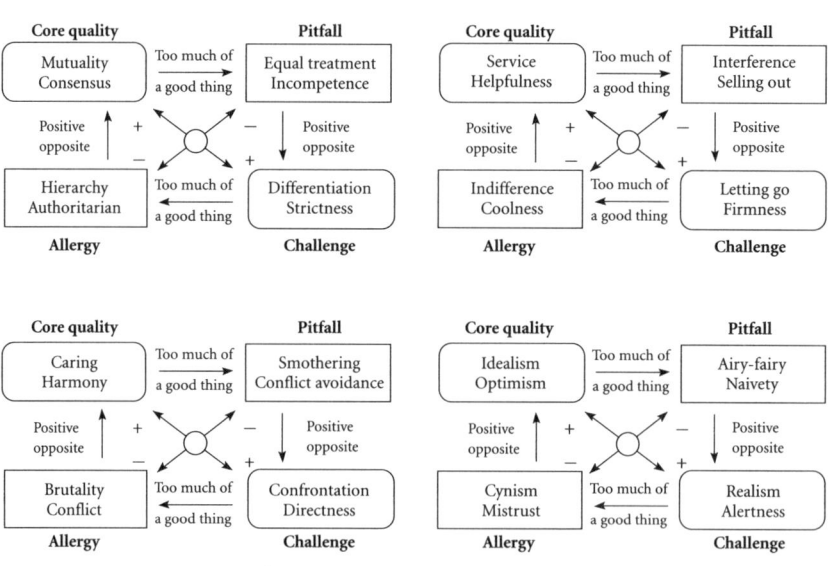

Core quadrants of the support oriented culture

106

oriented approach, particularly in professional organizations. Person-oriented cultures tend to envisage "Quality of Service" as carefully listening to the customer, being empathetic and going along with what the customer wants.

Cultural Analysis

Harrison's model may provide a very good idea of the various cultures, but it often raises this question: "All this is fine and well … but what do I do with it?" How can I, as a manager, increase my influence to create the culture I want? A cultural analysis can be a useful tool for answering this kind of question.

Cultural analysis is a *process instrument,* i.e. it is not primarily intended as a diagnostic method, but rather as a means to initiate a process of development within an organization. Its strength is that, when properly used, it mobilizes the *will* and creates *alignment.* This is most important in organizations that are not directly threatened from outside; or in organizations that do not see the immediate necessity of working on quality, "for things really aren't all that bad." These are often service organizations, partially state-controlled companies or "rich" companies (in a monopoly position).

As we said before, many organizations have *reactive* programs, programs launched to fight against something, the competition or demotivation. This means they are destined to be short-lived, because energy dissipates the moment the threat subsides. Since these programs aim to fight something, they will lose their oomph as soon they have "won." So, the end of the umpteenth program is guaranteed from the start. Cultural analysis, however, is a means to release *internal* energy, which is why it is mainly suited as a process instrument.

Before carrying out a culture analysis, management must clearly realize that this is not some method to satisfy their curiosity. A well-conducted cultural analysis *releases energy* in the organization. Since it is inevitable this will give rise to expectations, something must actually be done with the results. You cannot just stop after the analysis is finished. With cultural analyses, the question is no longer *if* you go on, but *how.* This makes it difficult for some managers to choose this approach. One feature of cultural analysis is that it is impossible to predict all the possible results. A cultural analysis is a choice for an *organic* approach, in other words that you simply set out on the road and cross bridges when you come to them. To a certain extent, this process can be directed by incorporating (or leaving out) certain habits. The important point is how the cultural analysis is structured and what fields of influence (on norms) are incorporated.

Norm Influence Areas

A norm influence area (on norms and values) is an area the culture of which is to be made the subject of discussion. Since cultural analysis is about mapping habits of behavior, a choice will have to be made during the preliminary stage of the analysis about which habits will (not) be included. There are countless ways of measuring habits. One could, for example, measure eating and sleeping habits, although it is very doubtful that this would be of any use. To determine what is useful, the *objective* of the cultural analysis must be known and an assessment made of the situation in that particular organization. This demonstrates that measuring and revealing corporate culture without having a clear goal in mind is generally not only useless, but also hopeless.

Conducting a cultural analysis only makes sense if a clear objective has been formulated.

This objective might be to discover obstacles to the introduction of quality management, but it could just as well be something else. We never use a standard questionnaire for analyzing corporate culture. The norm influence areas selected as the most important depend on the aim and nature of the organization. You could, for instance, bring the habits into the open that deal with "confrontation." This is accomplished by formulating statements that define this norm influence area.

When considering "confrontation," one might state the proposition, "It is a norm around here to smooth over problems," or "Management usually takes quick action when performance lags." Another proposition might be, "We normally avoid conflict so as not to rock the boat." Taken together, these propositions provide a picture of an organization's culture as far as confrontation is concerned. In this way, all fields are defined in a number of statements (usually four).

Whether a norm influence area is chosen depends on its relevance. If you want to implement a quality program, for example, it could be relevant to study habits of communication. Is communication between departments normal? Is communication usually one-way or two-way? Since effective communication is vital to the success of a quality program, it is a relevant field of study. Should the analysis show that communication in the organization is bad, it is doubtful that starting a quality program would be useful. Maybe something else needs to be done first.

The person conducting the analysis directs it by choosing the norm influence areas and the propositions, and can more or less decide which habits will be brought up for discussion. This makes it very easy to answer the question: is a cultural analysis scientific? Probably not, but that does not detract from its value. Cultural analysis is not a scientific *measuring* tool, it is a *process* tool, a means to discuss ingrained habits and determine together what to tackle or change. It generates *willpower* and *alignment,* and whether it is scientific or not is of secondary importance. One thing has become clear in practice: it works.

Cultural analyses are based on a number of interviews with a cross-section of the organization. This preliminary analysis attempts to establish the fields of influence that are worthwhile for this particular organization with this particular aim.

Implementation

A cultural analysis is not a survey; it is not a questionnaire which is sent to people, filled in and subsequently processed by a computer. Cultural analyses are carried out in workshops of about 12 people. All management levels always participate as well as 15 to 40 percent of the other staff. The reason why all management levels participate is that, to a large extent, they determine corporate culture, because they, more than anyone else, have the resources (and the power) to expect, encourage, reward or confront habits or behavior. Management workshops usually take a whole day, those for the non-executive staff half a day.

After a short introduction on organizational culture and on how a cultural analysis works, participants are asked to rate the propositions and use them to write a profile. Subsequently, an average group profile is made, so that everyone can see where and in what way he or she deviated from the average. The profile shows what the people doing the rating thought more or less usual.

Below you will find an example of a completed cultural profile of a commercial service organization with 900 employees with an internal and a field service. The aim of the cultural analysis was to compare the habits of the different sections of the field organization, to locate free energy, create unanimity and devise a plan of approach for the next two years.

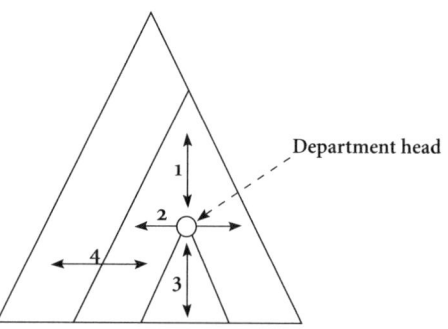

This organization chose to tackle four aspects in its cultural analysis. The first three sections concern the relation between branch management and department management (1); the next ten sections are concerned with their own level, with mutual relations between department managers (2); the seven sections following that are concerned with the relation between department managers and their subordinates (3); the last section deals with the relation between the field and internal services (4).

In this profile, a bold line indicates the average profile of branch management, and a thin line indicates the profile of an individual sector manager.

The value of such a profile is not determined by how high the scores are, but rather by the fact that a tool has been created to discuss systematically

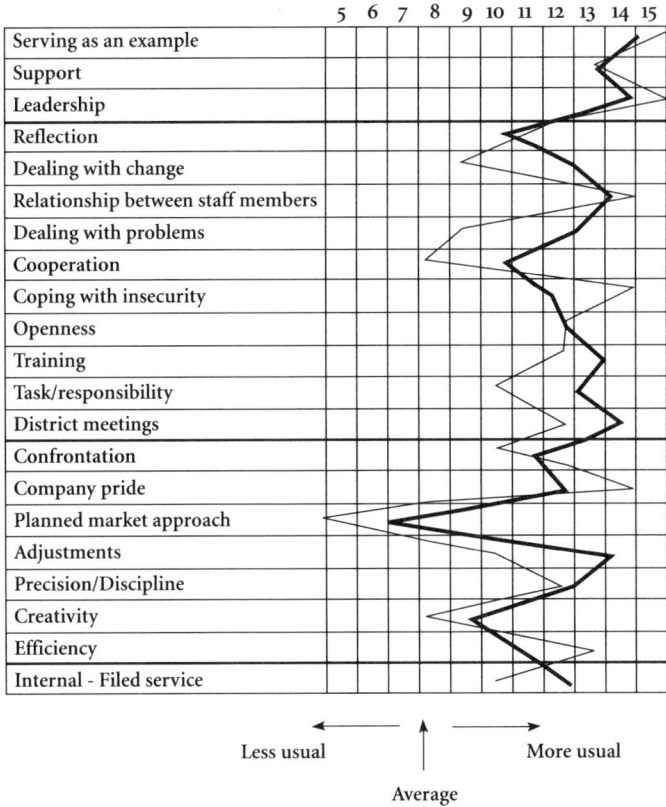

	5	6	7	8	9	10	11	12	13	14	15
Serving as an example											
Support											
Leadership											
Reflection											
Dealing with change											
Relationship between staff members											
Dealing with problems											
Cooperation											
Coping with insecurity											
Openness											
Training											
Task/responsibility											
District meetings											
Confrontation											
Company pride											
Planned market approach											
Adjustments											
Precision/Discipline											
Creativity											
Efficiency											
Internal - Filed service											

Less usual ← | ↑ | → More usual

Average

a number of issues. *The discussions generated by a cultural analysis are much more important than the actual profiles of the analyses.* During these discussions, participants gain insight into the existing culture and into the elements they want to keep or reinforce and those they would like to change. People will begin to see relationships between different fields, see the *compensating* mechanisms that have developed over the years to allow people to live with those aspects of corporate culture they do not really like. They will discover how all these habits are interrelated and kept intact. A process is set in motion within the organization that is potentially much more significant than the static picture provided by the cultural profile.

From Analysis to Action

All kinds of cross-sections of the organization can be made with these profiles. In the first of these, individuals from different levels of the

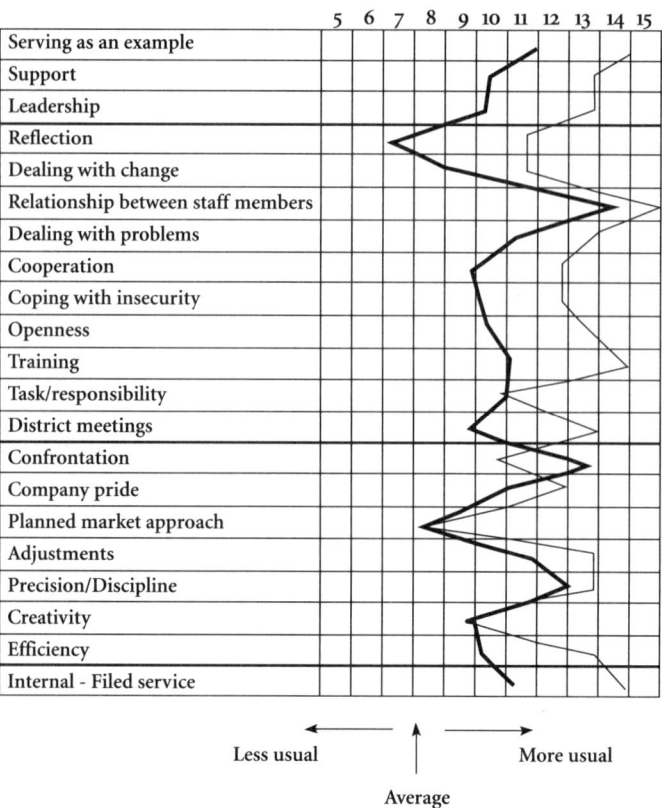

organization rate the propositions and together examine whether the lines of the profile run more or less *parallel* or mirror each other. If they mirror each other, the top of the organization has a different view of reality than the middle management (as is the case in the profile below). One might well conclude from this that the organization has a problem. The thin line represents a sector leader's profile, the bold line represents the average of the group of department heads he is in charge of.

One striking example is that the sector manager thinks it rather unusual for department heads to confront their subordinates (one of the lowest scores on his profile), while department heads consider this very usual (the second highest score in their profile). The point is not who is right, but that all concerned understand the thoughts underlying these profiles.

One of the pitfalls to be on guard against is drawing hasty conclusions about possible action. If you come to the conclusion together that systematic marketing is unusual, this does not necessarily mean anything. First of all, you should ask yourself what you want. Before any meaningful comment can be made on a profile, the *ideal profile,* outlining the ideal culture, must be drawn. This is not necessarily a straight line. The management usually draws up this ideal profile, which is why management workshops take a whole day instead of half a day.

Drawing up an ideal profile with non-executive staff can easily give rise to false hopes, and therefore potential advantages must first be weighed against the risks. By comparing the ideal profile with the real one, the biggest discrepancies between the ideal and the reality can be discovered and serve as points for further discussion.

Once the desired direction of development has been established, the question arises of what keeps the present culture intact, in other words, what the underlying support system is. As we have said before, culture exists because some habits are *expected, rewarded* and *encouraged.* This also goes for the habits we want to change. Apparently, these are also expected, rewarded and encouraged. How this actually occurs is explored with the participants.

They may come up with a story like the one below:

"Fire-fighting is typical, as can be seen from our profile. Looking ahead is uncommon with us, we score low on that one. Take meetings for example. If someone comes in fifteen minutes late, which happens regularly, the chairman first asks where he or she has been. The answer usually is that the person had something that needed doing right away. Then the chairman wants to know what it was. After explaining what it was and how urgent it was, he or she will often get a pat on the back. You will never hear the chairman (or anyone else) ask how this could have been avoided. You come in late, disturb the meeting, get attention, tell your story, and you get a pat on the back to boot. That's how it works with us…"

So is it surprising that time management training had not made the slightest difference in this case? Courses and training are useful only if something is also done about the underlying support system. If not, people will return to their old environment, where the old behavior is still expected, rewarded and encouraged.

The risk of cultural analysis is that people get hung up on generalities, especially when it comes to topics like communication. If that happens, participants must be "brought down to earth" by asking them questions like: How does this lack of communication manifest itself in practice? How can you tell if that is the case? How does it show? How can you make it more concrete? Can you define it so as to make it measurable? And so on.

This brings us back to concrete, everyday problems. The difference with the earlier situation is that participants are now *aware* that all their day-to-day worries, big or small, are not isolated incidents, but interrelated. Very often, it is clear that solutions are not to be found in the places they were usually sought. People realize that everyone is a cog in the machine, and that real change rarely "trickles down" from the top, but must start *inside* an organization.

Cultures and Qualities

Besides the above-mentioned ways of giving shape to the concept of organizational culture, you can also use core quadrants to examine the different qualities of groups, departments, divisions and organizations. They may give you a clearer idea of the challenges, pitfalls and allergies groups of people have.

For example, there was a multinational corporation that was planning to merge its Dutch and Belgian branches. Core quadrants were used to visualize the dynamics of this merger. First of all, different groups from both countries were asked to make a list of their own qualities and those of the other party (including pitfalls). The most striking thing was, that people always thought positively about themselves (core quality), and generally thought negatively about the other (allergy).

Prejudices abounded. The Dutch expressed these in remarks like "We are critical, while they are yes-men..." or "We are self-confident, they are submissive..." or "You cannot rely on Belgians—if they say yes, they may mean no..."

Remarks could be heard on the Belgian side such as: "We are flexible and they always have to point the finger…" or "We just take initiative and see if something works, while they always have endless discussions and deliberations about everything…" or "The Dutch are always so pushy…"

After this, both parties were invited to work out their remarks in core quadrants. The Dutch groups came up with the following core quadrants, which showed that their challenge always turned out to be the Belgians' core quality.

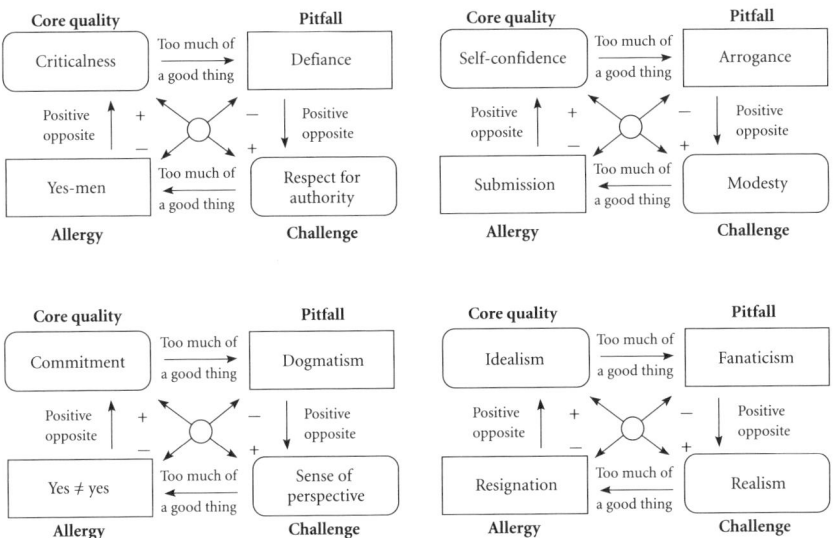

Core quadrants of and by the Dutch

The Belgian employees of this company were asked to do the same, but vice versa. To everyone's surprise, the Belgians' challenges all turned out to be the Dutch' core qualities.

During the making of these core quadrants it became clear in both countries that this merger might be very fruitful, because both groups could learn a great deal from each other.

They also discovered that, in a way, they were allergic to each other, which left them with the choice between either fighting each other or cooperating.

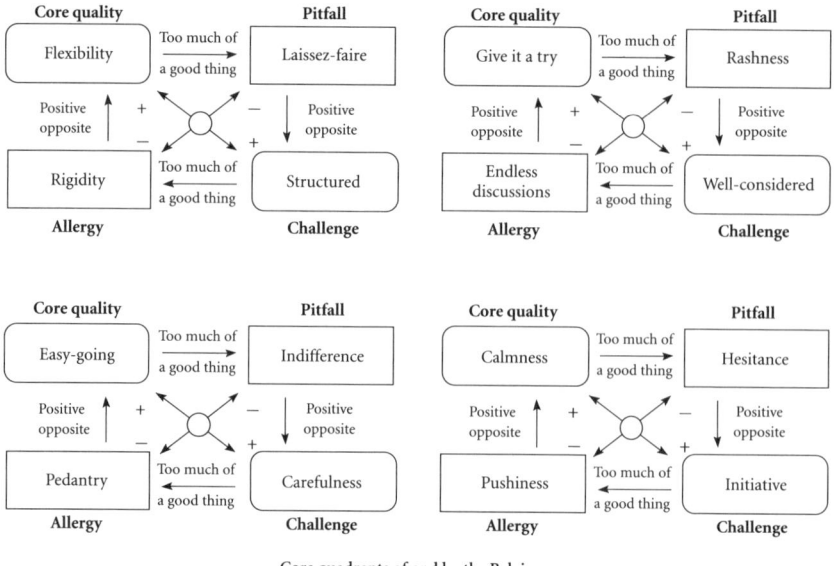

Core quadrants of and by the Belgians

By having the two groups exchange experiences, they grew to respect each other more and dislike (allergy) each other less.

In this way, potential conflicts during mergers can be recognized early on and (sometimes) neutralized. It certainly makes it easier to anticipate possible mutual rejection mechanisms.

Two insurance companies that were to merge concluded that their core qualities would complement each other beautifully. One party's core quality was obedience, the other's independence. The ideas people in both organizations had about each other were less positive, however. The people in the first organization thought the others high-handed, those in the second thought the others subservient and servile.

Worked out in a double core quadrant, these differences are obvious. The double quadrant shows these are companies with complementary qualities, which can either cooperate successfully or get bogged down by unproductive reproaches and infighting.

This method of analyzing culture is particularly suitable if you want to stress the relation between the "I" approach and the "We" approach. What's more, learning about core qualities in this way invites people to

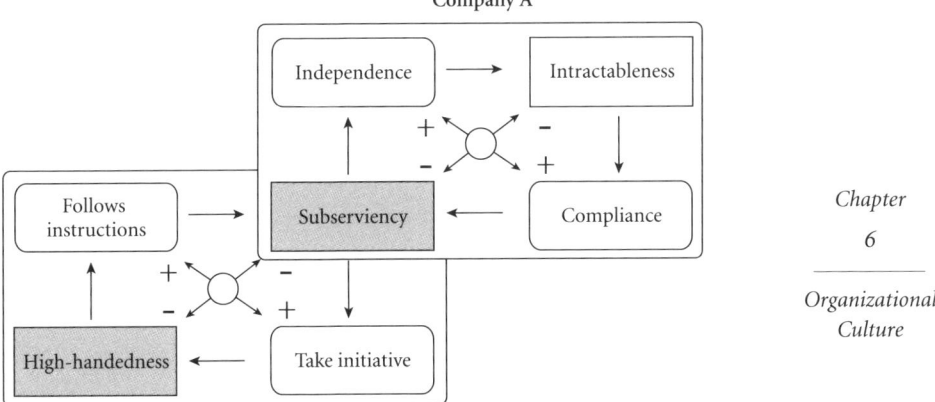

Company A

Company B

apply them individually and makes it clear that personal development and organizational development influence each other, and that an organization can never develop further than its leader.

The new general manager of a—financially—successful company wanted to give the company new momentum. A preliminary survey showed that the company improvised very well, but that it was rather unstructured. People found it very difficult to know when and where to draw the line. Exceeding budgets, missing deadlines, very few confrontations, and no job assessments or performance reviews were just a few symptoms of this. There was literally no line drawn around the premises (no fence), so that everyone could take goods, tools and raw materials to their heart's desire, which they did on a large scale.

This company's weakness was clearly its "boundlessness," yet it achieved good results. It was obvious that a more structured way of working was necessary. In the past, however, all attempts at this had never got past the good-resolutions stage. Everybody agreed that a change was called for, but when it came to the crunch, everyone turned a deaf ear and always found excuses why it was once again not necessary. Set out in a core quadrant, the cultural problem was crystal clear.

In a workshop, the management team decided to formulate tasks and work in a planned and structured manner. It was very important that

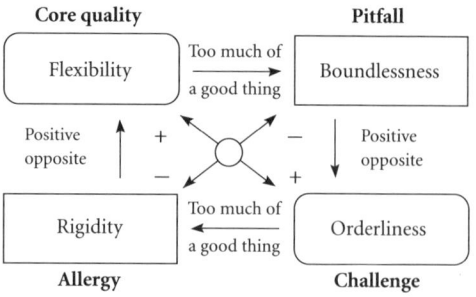

they went through the process of choice (which we discussed earlier). All participants found it very hard to actually make a choice. Every time things threatened to become concrete, people tried to stand back and look at them from a different perspective or water them down. For most, departing from the old ways of doing things was far from easy. After weighing the pros and cons for a long time, a choice was finally made.

The first step, they decided, was to approach problems systematically. It was clear this would meet with quite a lot of resistance in the organization and that it would be dismissed as overly rigid (allergy). To overcome this difficulty, four strategic projects were initiated by means of a Project Start Up and introduced to the organization by the general manager/ project initiator as examples of the new direction and way of working. These activities were not what could be called spectacular, it was mainly the combination of understanding the culture (the "We" side), the personal commitment of key figures (the "I" side) and the structure provided by systematic working (the "It" side) that finally lead to a breakthrough in the organization.

Culture and Subpersonalities

Finally, a playful way to reveal culture is to use subpersonalities. The various dominant subpersonalities in an organization can be given shape and worked out in groups.

One U.S. sales organization identified the "Midwest Farmer," the "Inventor" and the "Controller" as strong subpersonalities. By creating a caricature of each of these subpersonalities and having these carry on a discussion, a clear picture emerged of the source of both alignment and confusion in the organization. It also became clear how the people in the organization always managed to find the "perfect" excuse. It was amazing to see that people managed to sell their faults and shortcomings in such a way as to even receive a pat on the back. People proved to know intuitively which subpersonality to use to get their way. Consciously choosing no longer to use ready-made excuses to get out of living up to agreements can dramatically increase an organization's creative power.

As with individuals, collective subpersonalities carry both a positive message (something they stand for) and a caricature in which they exaggerate wildly, thinking only they are important or, going to the opposite extreme, sacrificing themselves completely.

Creative organizations are culture-oriented. For a manager, this means understanding how culture works, is maintained and can be created from inside (himself). The more managers are aware of their own core qualities and act upon them, the better they will be able to bring about a creative culture through effective choices.

⁷] Managing Transitions

Listening is easy.
Remembering is harder.
Letting go is the hardest of all.

Different Kinds of Transitions

With or without a cultural analysis, the road to a creative organization is certain to be paved with major and minor transitions. It may be useful to ask yourself which kind of transition you are actually going through.

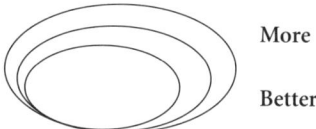

More

Better

If it is about doing something better or having more of the same, the impact on the organization is likely to be small. Logical and rational thinking can deal with these kinds of changes very well. It gets quite a bit more difficult when we are dealing with something that, although familiar, is new to us. On the one hand, we envisage the new reality clearly, on the other, we have to wait and see if it will turn out that way.

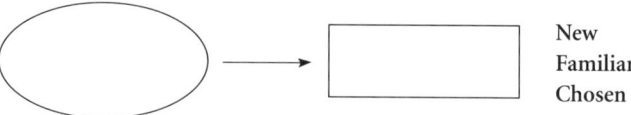

New
Familiar
Chosen

The most difficult transitions are those to a new and unknown situation, when it is unclear what exactly the new reality will look like. These are also called transformations.

In reality, situations are often initially thought of as new and familiar, while, in retrospect, they prove to have been transformations.

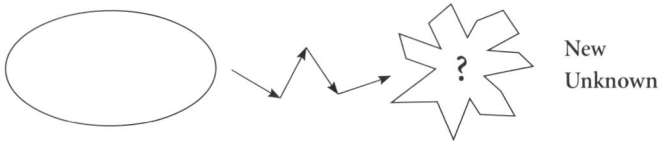

I am fully convinced that transitions of this kind will be characteristic of the near future. Today's problems require that new and unknown avenues be explored and followed. If we continue to do more of the same, we continue to create more of the same crises. In the mid-eighties there was talk of a "transformation boom." Transformation management was new and attracted a lot of attention. At the time, I distanced myself from this movement, because I believe transformation is not something you can plan. The most you can do is conclude after the fact that a fundamental change has taken place. As far as I am concerned, transformation can and should never be an objective. What matters is leadership that dares take a leap in the dark if the organization should need it. Later, we'll see whether this can be termed a transformation or not.

Phases Occurring During Transitions

Typically, managers deal with change or transitions by concerning themselves with what is new, they rarely ask themselves questions about what is past, what is over, questions about the end of the "old." Jack Tesmer believes managing transitions means first understanding that you are dealing with two simultaneous processes, each governed by its own laws. To facilitate the transition, managers must of course have a clear image, in terms of character behavior (behavioral culture), of the new situation they see emerging. What behavior will correspond with the new reality? A cultural analysis can be a useful tool for reaching a consensus on this issue within the organization.

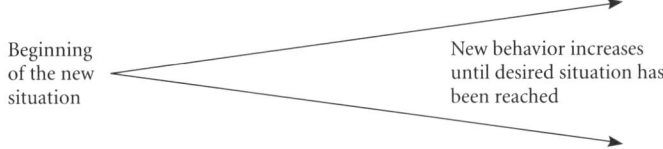

Beginning of the new situation

New behavior increases until desired situation has been reached

It is equally important to have a clear picture of what will cease to exist in the future. In other words, which present reality (in terms of behavior) are we departing from? What is over, won't be there anymore, is a thing of the past? What is often regarded as "resistance to change" is actually the natural human reaction to letting go of something familiar and known. As we said before, this is not simply a matter of turning a switch, not for individuals, let alone for groups or organizations.

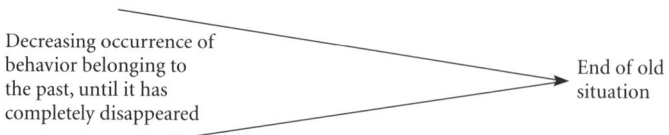

Decreasing occurrence of behavior belonging to the past, until it has completely disappeared

End of old situation

In unconscious transitions, the two above-mentioned processes overlap, creating four phases that are recognizable to some extent in all transitions, depending on the nature and scope of the change. Jack Tesmer distinguishes the following phases in transition processes:

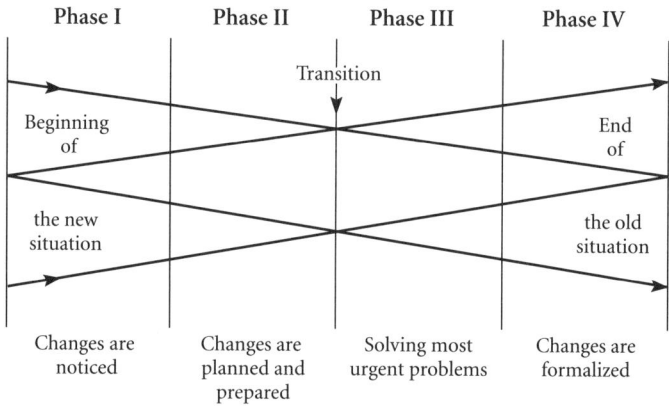

Tesmer's model of transition

In phase I, the first hints of change in the environment become noticeable. A culture's natural reaction will be to protect itself against an uncertain future. It is not unusual for people to deny any change is coming, "Oh, but it won't really happen…" Energy is directed inward and people are mostly concerned with their own affairs. As demonstrated by the curve plotting the individual's acceptance process, feelings of insecurity and impotence may be aroused. People tend to look to and become dependent on outside direction. They are generally less prepared to take risks and have greater problems expressing their feelings.

In phase II, preparations are made for the "necessary" change. Intensity increases. If the aim and purpose of the change remain unclear, productivity will decline. If people feel they cannot contribute to plans and decisions, these feelings can easily degenerate into opposition and aggression. People become more reactive. At the point of transition from the old situation to the new one, people have to deal with both. At this point, people experiencing an unconscious transition reach the lowest point in the curve.

In phase III, the first problems springing from this change must be tackled. It is a period of practical adjustment, in which people grapple with new structures, systems and/or new co-workers. They are mainly concerned with trying to discover what the new reality entails, while they still have one foot in the old situation.

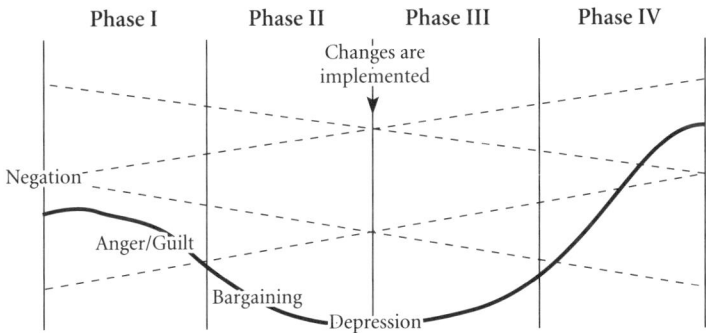

At the point the organization most needs its people's active contribution, they (who are in the middle of an unconscious transition) are often least prepared to give it, because they may be experiencing a bout of depression.

If things turn out better than expected, the energy level will begin to pick up and people will search for new opportunities in the new reality.

In phase IV, the changes are formalized and integrated into the new systems and structures, while the old cease to exist. People work from their core qualities (again), creativity can be expressed (again), and reactivity diminishes.

Managing Transitions

As many managers know, unconscious or undirected transitions can be long, frustrating and costly in terms of productivity and motivation. Nor is it unusual for people to realize afterwards that they have learned a great deal from it. Conscious transition management means the manager will influence the process, though not in the sense of trying to control it completely, which is impossible on the way to an uncertain future, anyway. He or she exerts influence in the sense of realizing that the process of psychological acceptance people are going through can (and must) be accelerated. This is necessary in order to prepare people for the impending change and enable them to go through their own process, so that they will actually be available the moment the organization needs them the most.

This means that the process of psychological transition is complete the moment the change is actually implemented. To achieve this, the manager will have to do his best to communicate everything he knows and does not know about the impending change during phase I. In this phase, openness and honesty are of paramount importance, particularly when it comes

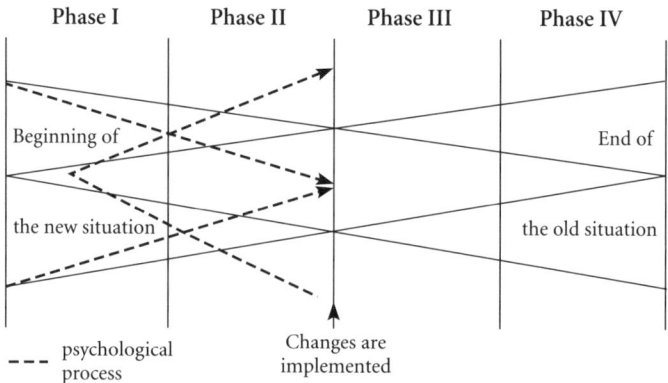

to "not knowing" things, because often people have the idea that "they" do know something they're not telling.

In the second phase, the emphasis is on maximum opportunity for input and involvement in the preparations and plans for the change. By constantly re-focusing attention on the higher aims, the utility and necessity of these changes, people are invited to become co-creators of the new future. The moment people realize how their individual choices (can) contribute to the future situation, they will become more willing to participate. In creative organizations, all levels shape the future, and the management's task is to act as both guide and midwife.

8] From a Reactive Organization to a Creative one

Three Frames of Reference

To describe the three stages of the development process from a reactive to a creative organization, I like to refer to the work of Linda Nelson and Frank L. Burns.[1] This chapter is an adaptation of their work, including a few changes in terminology and supplements referring to previous chapters.

The work of Nelson and Burns is fascinating because they describe a four-stage development process, from a reactive organization to a responsive and proactive organization, finally to a high-performance culture. I have reduced this to a three-stage process: from a reactive to a responsive organization, and then to a creative organization. These different categories can be regarded as frames of reference within which the people in an organization think and act. Each frame of reference builds upon the previous one, extending and refining it. A grasp of these frames of reference may help us understand how the organization functions at the moment, and what we can do to make it a creative organization. Below, you will find an outline of the features of organizations in various stages.

The Reactive Organization

The reactive organization is at the bottom of the development spiral, because it has not yet really started on the road to a creative organization. Reactive organizations are hardly ever, if at all, focused on external results or performance. The organization is very much centered upon itself. It is not so much the starting point of a development as a situation organizations slip into.

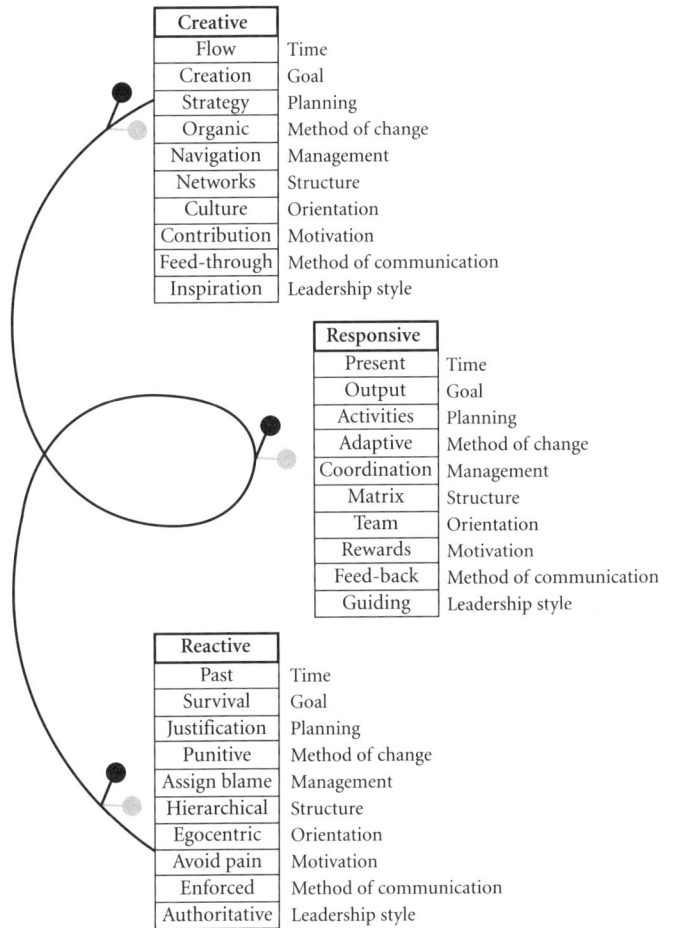

Creative	
Flow	Time
Creation	Goal
Strategy	Planning
Organic	Method of change
Navigation	Management
Networks	Structure
Culture	Orientation
Contribution	Motivation
Feed-through	Method of communication
Inspiration	Leadership style

Responsive	
Present	Time
Output	Goal
Activities	Planning
Adaptive	Method of change
Coordination	Management
Matrix	Structure
Team	Orientation
Rewards	Motivation
Feed-back	Method of communication
Guiding	Leadership style

Reactive	
Past	Time
Survival	Goal
Justification	Planning
Punitive	Method of change
Assign blame	Management
Hierarchical	Structure
Egocentric	Orientation
Avoid pain	Motivation
Enforced	Method of communication
Authoritative	Leadership style

From a reactive to a creative organization

Characteristically, people in these organizations do not or no longer experience a sense of common purpose, nor do they feel they achieve anything. In reactive organizations, the original aim has lost its vitality; there is no longer any inspiration. The organization floats around aimlessly and confused, just busy surviving. Since people have no clear sense of their aim, they cannot concentrate on the future, and their attention gets caught up in the *past* more and more.

The energy is reactive and directed against something; it is neither vital nor aligned. Superficially, the structure of reactive organizations still appears to be well-organized. Below the surface, however, it often has fragmented into (sub)parts that fight or compete with each other. By producing reports, papers and memos, managers lead people to believe that they are making a constant effort to locate and solve problems. They focus on structure and controlling people and resources. Instead of solving the problem, people are corrected or punished. Communication takes the shape of orders passed down by a divided hierarchy, which causes a defensive atmosphere in the organization, with people primarily trying to protect themselves and concentrating on avoiding problems. They no longer dare stick out their neck and they try to gloss over any mistakes.

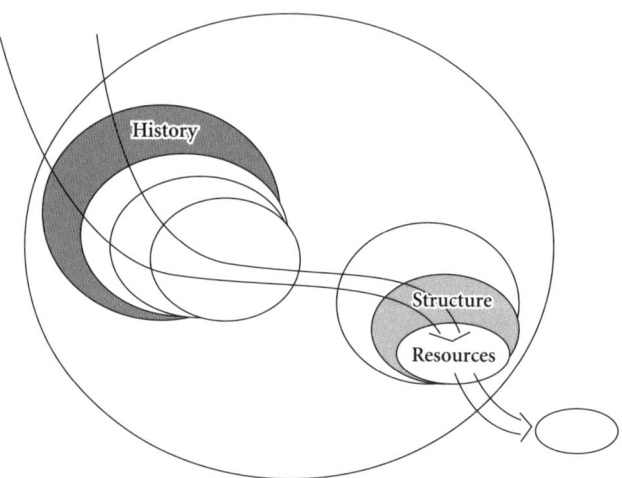

The Reactive Organization

Masking behavior is everywhere. Choices are ineffective because they are reactive, provisional, and do not contribute to the whole (egocentric); nor are they rooted in fundamental choices (vision); they are conditional and often exceed the limits of authority people have for action.

In reactive organizations, willingness to undergo real changes is often minimal, because these threaten to change the rules of survival people have learned the hard way, and this would further endanger their already shaky sense of security. The above is a description of how such a "no risk" organization remains intact.

128

Developing a Reactive Organization

To change a reactive organization into a responsive one, a manager must strike the ideal balance between patience and perseverance, since not only the individual employee's frame of reference must be changed, but also that of the organization as a whole. The organization's aims must be explained and mutual trust built up between management and personnel. The best way to do this is by linking aims with actual projects, because these can be accurately formulated, thereby giving all parties something to go by. In this way, a feeling of common purpose can be created which will lend the organization new vitality and energy.

Reactive	Responsive	
	Present	Time
Past	Output	Goal
Survival	Activities	Planning
Justification	Adaptive	Method of change
Punitive	Coordination	Management
Assign blame	Matrix	Structure
Hierarchy	Team	Orientation
Egocentric	Rewards	Motivation
Avoid pain	Feed-back	Method of communication
Enforced	Guiding	Leadership style
Authoritative		

To achieve this, meetings can be organized for goal-setting and planning activities. Not only the management must be present at these meetings, but also the workers. At the lower levels, developing the "It side" must first be emphasized. Attention should also be paid to team-building, by developing creative problem-solving abilities (see chapter 11).

Working together on concrete activities is highly conducive to creating clarity and mutual trust. In addition, active participation in the solving of problems that arise in the organization must be encouraged, for example by setting up quality teams (see chapter 10). Besides the added benefit of training employees in problem solving, they learn to watch closely for any signs of them. Here too, the principle is put into practice that those responsible for applying the solution to a problem must also be involved in inventing it.

In a nutshell, a reactive organization can strike out in a more responsive direction by:

- Setting goals
- Planning activities
- Solving problems both creatively and analytically
- Performance management (appreciation and confrontation)
- Developing creative problem solving abilities

The Responsive Organization

The responsive organization is characterized by its focus on present output. The work is carried out by (project) teams (see Chapter 9), whose members help in the development of aims and planning activities and, therefore, know exactly what is expected and what must be done to achieve them. There is a positive feeling of team spirit and members do their best for themselves and for the organization. More energy is released.

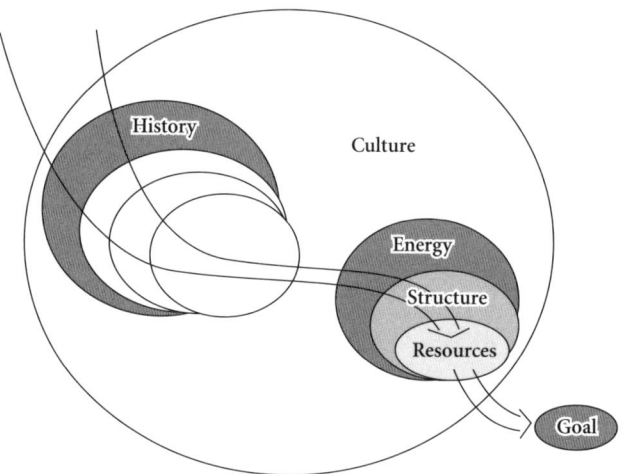

The Responsive Organization

The manager is a coach who motivates his team by making plans, keeping the team's goals alive and giving positive feedback if performance is good. He will not settle for results that are below par, but will confront and appreciate his team and focus all energy on their goal. In responsive organizations, the focus is still on the short-term and often limited to the separate aims of separate activities. The bigger picture, i.e. the philosophy and vision employees, teams and departments can use as a frame of reference is still lacking. The creative organization provides such a frame of reference.

Developing a Responsive Organization

To develop a responsive organization into a creative one, a clear "future," a vision must first be created. People cannot be *proactive* if they do not know where they are heading. This vision of the future must be generally accepted throughout the organization and be so inspiring that people are prepared to do their very best for it.

A second important step is making clear that the organization greatly *values* its people. Greater emphasis on important values will make people feel more part of the whole, and they will regard the organization as an extension of themselves. Besides alignment, attunement is also necessary. An organization's performance as a whole depends on that of all individual members. The management constantly tries to convey this message, not just in words but also by their actions. Core quadrants and focusing on personal core qualities ("I" side) can provide an impetus for attunement.

Responsive	Creative	
	Flow	Time
Present	Creation	Goal
Output	Strategy	Planning
Activities	Organic	Method of change
Adaptive	Navigation	Management
Coordination	Networks	Structure
Matrix	Culture	Orientation
Team	Contribution	Motivation
Rewards	Feed-through	Method of communication
Feed-back	Inspiration	Leadership style
Guiding		

The third important element is that the mission and the vision developed by the organization not be directed merely at the organization itself, but that they be linked to more general human or social values, connecting the organization's activities to a higher level of meaning. Mission and vision serve as a foundation for the organization's choices. On the basis of such a vision, the organization can start developing a long-term strategy.

Clearly stated, fully accepted values and a vision of the future based on them, serve as the glue that keeps the organizational culture together. In a nutshell, a responsive organization can strike out in a more creative direction by:

- Formulating a mission and a vision
- Explicitly stating the most important values
- Long-term planning
- Developing the organization's human resources by learning to recognize, value and appreciate the core qualities of individuals and departments.

The Creative Organizational Culture

Founded on a value-based philosophy, creative organizations work on and towards the future. Proactive organizations regard their own future as a *choice* to be made and not as a given that they will have to learn to live with. Creative organizations focus on long-term results and the strategies

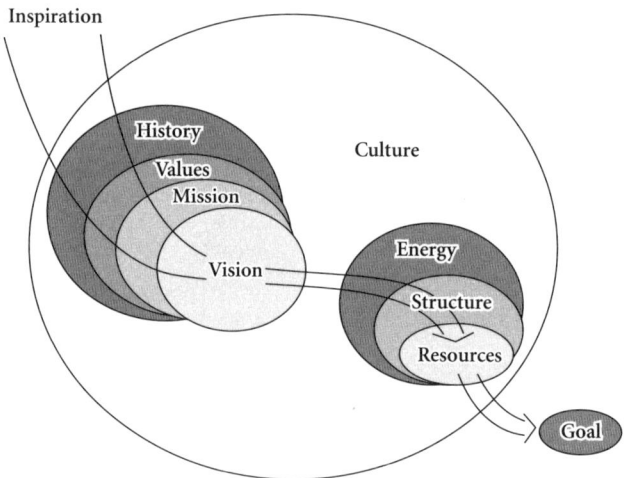

The Creative Organization

to achieve them. Change is planned by the management and used to enhance organizational efficiency. Attention is paid to the effects of the present situation on the plans for the future.

Members of the organization are motivated because they can contribute to the realization of a future they value, and form part of a close team working in a common direction.

Leaders of proactive organizations reinforce this culture by keeping the organization on course to its target, and especially by the style with which they do this. They know how to calculate risks and to welcome change in the organization as an opportunity for further growth and development. To do this, leaders must be able to build up relationships with their co-workers characterized by trust and mutual support. One feature of this leadership style is clear mutual respect and loyalty.

Development of creative organizations is further stimulated by teaching all individuals to make their own choices (attuned and aligned), appealing to each individual's sense of complete responsibility for themselves.

Leaders view themselves first and foremost as managers of human energy and vitality, which is used to constantly seek new possibilities and opportunities for the organization. An understanding of these matters enables them to continually re-adjust the organization's aim and task.

Strategic choices are made on the basis of a philosophy that gives meaning and "sense" to long-term plans. Managing a creative organization also involves making plans for its continuing development; material growth is regarded as an expression of inner growth.

Another aspect of the creative organization is its stress on the development of "metasystems" such as quality teams and networks. Creative leaders do not just concentrate on realizing the potential of their own organization and its members, they also consider their organization's role in society and regard it as an instrument to contribute to the community as a whole.

In this frame of reference, leadership primarily serves as a "direction-seeking instrument," in constant interaction with the flow of developments in the world. Leaders embody a combination of past, present and future: they respect tradition, are very well-informed about the present situation and have a clear vision of the future. For that reason, they do not think of change as a threat, but as the only certainty there is. Their task, therefore, is not reducing, fighting or controlling change, but managing it.

Creative cultures appreciate the importance of ceremonies and ritual and of positive legends contributing to the idea of a rich heritage that must be respected and carried on. Such cultures stimulate both management and employees to aim to fulfill their potential inside the organization, and not to restrict this to activities outside it. Leaders leave their people free to pursue the vision upon which the organization is founded, and also give them power and responsibility so that they have the energy and the opportunity for adventure, creativity and innovation.

Part Three

A Closer Look at the Main Themes

9] The Project Approach

Why Do We Now Need a "Project Approach" to Work?

Modern times are characterized by the challenges posed by the rapid changes in politics, technology and society, in which themes like *diversification, integration* and *individualization* play a major role.

As we said before, technological developments in telecommunications, satellite TV and computer networks direct society towards increasing interdependence and integration, simultaneously creating more chances, choices and opportunities for the individual. Access to increasing information and knowledge gives people new opportunities for personal development.

The same trends are perceptible in business and (commercial) services: interdependence, diversification and integration. In many organizations, the "walls" between departments are felt to be one of the biggest stumbling blocks to positive results. People feel the need for "permeable walls." Increasing interdependence makes *solidarity between people* increasingly important. Society's growing complexity requires individuals to take more responsibility and initiative at the personal level and assume a less cautious and reserved attitude. Efficient anticipation of developments requires quicker and more direct methods of cooperation, just as increasing time pressure requires an approach that cuts *through* existing structures and cuts *out* all bureaucracy.

That is precisely why a "project approach" to work is enjoying such interest at the moment. It is a logical and fitting answer to the far-reaching developments and changes of today.

"The Project Approach:" The Traditional Theory

The "project approach" was originally a form of the "plan approach," with work being systematically structured to strive for a *result* that was consciously chosen in advance. Using the project approach, one imposes restrictions on oneself in order to reach the optimum result.

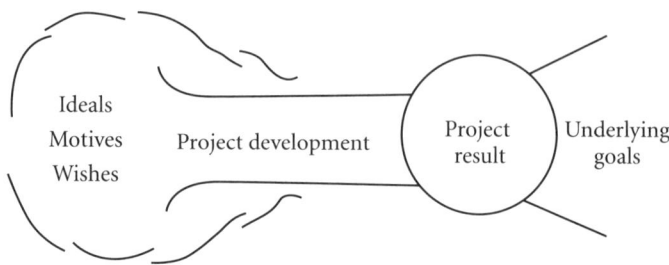

The four basic principles of this system are:

- Formulating
- Phasing
- Deciding
- Controlling

Formulating the project result means formulating the problem and determining what the project should and should not comprise.

Phasing means charting the course towards the result and dividing this into logical and manageable "stages," so that the complex whole is divided into well-defined and coherent task components.

Deciding means: the point during the process when we coordinate matters with the client and the critical decisions involved.

Controlling means attending to the controlling aspects of time, money, quality, information and organization. These five controlling aspects offer the opportunity to build in guarantees to make and keep the project well-organized and manageable.

Every project has a *commissioner* who ensures that the results match the original wishes and expectations. The initiator is the one who receives the results of the project (on behalf of the organization, the environment or the users). This person makes sure to accomplish one or more aims.

One encounters a clearly discernible "masculine" quality in the language and images of this (also see the figure above). The project approach has the image of being a strictly controlled way of working: the situation is well in hand, nothing left to chance, and the result is sacred.

If distorted, this can degenerate into an attempt to force results, leaving no leeway for peace, responsiveness, caring or reflection. The more "feminine" qualities are actually denied and/or suppressed.

"The Project Approach:" The Real Theory

It is becoming increasingly evident that the project approach to work is much more than just a system. In essence, it means creating something together; *it is a way of collectivizing the individual creative process.*

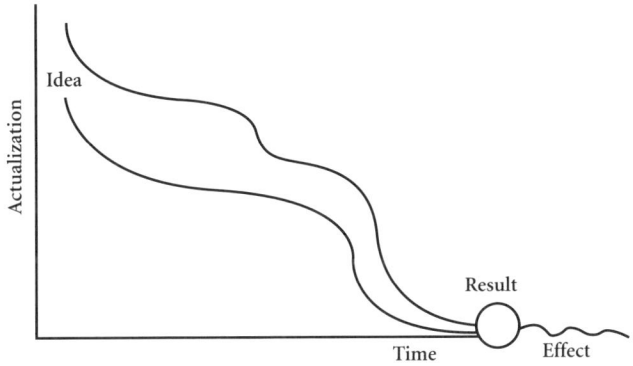

'The Project Approach' as a creative process

A concrete result materializes in time from the world of ideas, a result which will have a certain impact on the environment. Viewed in this way, the question that must be constantly asked is how to make the environment in which the result will have to operate responsive. If no one starts thinking about this until the result has arrived, you might say the organization is "raped."

By looking at this method as if it were a collective creative process, thoughts on result and process will become more balanced. After all, they are both important. Whereas individuals used to be capable of creating something alone (by making choices), interdependence and interrelation now cause people to (have to) go through this process together.

Another interesting point is that, although the age of the pharaohs gave rise to great creations, at that time, in contrast to the present, it was possible to use violence to force people to make an effort. The result was not influenced by people relating, or not relating, to each other and what they were doing. Considering the nature of the efforts demanded of people today, this is now unthinkable.

Formulating the project result creates tension in the organization. Collectively, the organization undertakes to accomplish a goal set in advance. The rules and regulations pertaining to "Wishing versus Choosing," which we discussed in chapter 3, apply here, too. The process for arriving at a well-chosen project result should consist of the same steps:

1   Listening: "What do I want (as an organization)?"
2   Finding direction by formulating your wish in the form of a result.
3   Examining the present reality.
4   Checking the effectiveness of the possible choice.
5   Choosing to achieve the result within a fixed period of time.
6   Following process development

Checking a chosen project result's effectiveness is particularly important with this approach:

- Checking reactivity
- Checking contribution
- Checking embedment
- Checking conditionality
- Checking responsibility for action
- Checking consequences

Some attempts are now being made to incorporate *reflection* into the "project approach" to work. Reflection means regularly taking a step back to look at what effect the project result is meant to have (contribution in the long term).

Making collective choices can enhance the entire organization's creative power. In the long run, however, this will work only if all individuals in the organization start expressing their individual creativity.

Thus, the project approach is not just a different way of working, but a different way of thinking, one that demands a different kind of consciousness. This is particularly true of the project leader. The present project leader may be a forerunner of the future leader; it is clear in any case that most organizations do not back a project leader's responsibilities with formal authority. He or she is supposed to get things done without having any authority to fall back on. This inevitably means project leaders must rely solely on their own resources and core qualities. If a project leader cannot be inspired from within, he will mostly be doomed to become frustrated and overworked.

Once learned, the effects of the project approach are also felt outside of the project itself. People become more result-oriented; greater clarity is created and, consequently, a greater understanding of how projects function. Cooperative ties are established and/or reinforced. Individual commitment to and unity with the organization become stronger and stronger. This makes the project approach an excellent way to initiate a development process in an organization, a process to which the three essential aspects of change processes in organizations once again apply:

'It' side
Formulating
Phasing
Deciding
Controlling

The Project Approach

'We' side
Cooperation
Team spirit
Identity
Culture

'I' side
Project leadership
Responsibility
Core qualities
Reflection & Inspiration

The "It" side is concerned with the systematic aspect of the project approach that has proved its worth in practice. It is also what the project approach is known for.

During the last ten years, the "We" side of this method has emerged as a factor that, to a large extent, determines the final result. Some examples of questions of cooperation are:

- How can we maximize project teams' chances of success in the existing organizational culture?
- How can we understand the power in and around the project?
- How can we optimize the interrelation between the project team and the organization?
- How can we put together a good team?
- How do we generate team spirit?

Until now, the "I" side of the project approach has remained greatly underestimated and underdeveloped. As we have said before, project leaders are an outstanding example of individuals whose influence must be derived from their *personality*, because their hierarchical power is usually limited. It is precisely this kind of situation in which concern for inner processes and insight into one's own and other people's core qualities play such a vital role in inspiring project team leadership and making effective choices.

The project approach to improving primary processes lends new *vitality* to organizations; it unites people's core qualities and the organization's strengths and capitalizes on them.

10] Quality

There is no Power
in all of Creation
greater than Love…

Quality in Service Companies

Quality is a concept that has received widespread attention since the mid-eighties. Companies and people everywhere are asking themselves how to improve the quality of their service: banks, insurance companies, administrative offices, to name but a few. What is the source of all this interest in service quality? One of the causes may be the results of a survey that was conducted in the U.S. and Canada a few years ago, inquiring into customers' reasons for changing rather than returning to their former suppliers or service organizations. The results are absolutely remarkable. The survey produced the following facts:

  1 percent dies or retires
  3 percent changes jobs or address
  5 percent patronizes friends/acquaintances
  9 percent tries the competition
 14 percent is dissatisfied with product or service
 68 percent *rejects supplier's indifferent attitude*

This means that in 68 percent of all cases the service organization's indifferent *attitude* is to blame for customers not returning, while in only 23 percent of all cases (9 percent + 14 percent) product or service-related factors are to blame. Add to this the fact that the complaints registered by the organization itself usually concern the 23 percent and hardly ever the 68 percent, and the figures are even more telling. They also tell why the maxim "dissatisfied customers do not complain, they go elsewhere," is especially true in the service industry. It is understandable that customers will not easily complain about a service organization's attitude, because this is a matter of perception rather than an objectively measurable fact. These figures underline that quality in service is primarily a matter of *contact* or *connection*.

That the service industries have only recently become interested in quality is partly due to the fact that concepts about quality originate in production companies. Goods are produced in one place and consumed in another (e.g. at home). Customers experience the quality of goods usually in their own environment, while the quality of services is usually experienced in the environment of the person or institution providing the service (e.g. at the front desk). Making a distinction between production and services we can conclude that:

- Goods are produced
- Services are rendered.

In the service industry, production and consumption often coincide, both in time and in place. The customer experiences the quality of a telephone conversation as either good or bad at the moment it is taking place; a bad service, unlike an article, cannot be exchanged. That "quality experience" plays an important role in service is expressed clearly in the common expression "You never get a second chance to make a first impression."

Service is mainly an interactive process between the customer and the person/institution rendering the service, which makes it highly individual. If a customer is dissatisfied with a product, he can exchange it or receive his money back. It is characteristic of services that customers usually do not take home anything tangible, except a piece of paper. They may be paying for a future promise, as with an insurance policy. What's more, a service can rarely be demonstrated or displayed to show the customer how good it is. This makes quality in service a complex question, and it explains why it did not become a topic of current interest until the mid-eighties.

The History of Quality

I think it may be useful to give an outline of the most important "quality gurus" and their messages, particularly so that we may recognize the direction in which thinking about quality has developed.

Listing the four most well-known gurus, we get the following picture:

Guru	Message	Concerns	System
Deming	To measure is to know	Specialist	Quality Control
Juran	There is always room for improvement	Manager	Quality Management
Crosby	Get it right the first time	Management	Quality Care
Ishikawa	Listen to people	Employee	Quality Circles

The concept of "quality" has come to have a broader and broader meaning over the past few decades. Whereas the emphasis was first placed on statistical analysis techniques, today's thinking focuses more on processes of organizational change, management philosophy and consciousness-raising.

Thus, quality is not a new concept. The first attempt at quality assurance was to conduct quality audits at the end of the (production) process. Inspections occurred *afterwards,* and if products did not satisfy the requirements they were rejected. Although this method limited the risk of customers' getting bad products/services, it did not lead to continuous quality improvement. It was an accepted part of the production process that x percent was below par, and as long as they did not exceed the x percent mark, everything was fine. Or, as Dr. Juran so aptly puts it: "As long as they stayed below the norm, the alarm bells were switched off."

Later, people realized more and more that quality is not something you can add afterwards, but the result of a process in which everything is *done right the first time.* This means everyone should be constantly striving for improvement, until everything is done right the first time. Eventually, audits should become superfluous. To arrive at this point, managers have to eliminate two persistent misconceptions:

- Quality takes time and therefore it will only cost money.
- People are dumb and uninterested.

The persistence of these misconceptions is evident from the fact that similar remarks can still be heard today in many organizations. In many places people came to see things differently by asking themselves the question "Why is it that we always have time to do things over again, but never have time to get them right the first time?" By listening to suggestions for improvement from the workfloor, many companies have discovered over the years that those who do the work on a daily basis will often have very good ideas of how it can be done better and more practically.

The first thing that comes to mind when thinking about quality is quality standards to determine the requirements that processes and people have to meet to become a smoothly functioning whole. However, "standardization projects" in the service industry still rarely end up producing the desired effect. Many standards are set, but this does not mean they are met. Quality in service industries involves a lot more than adhering to standards. They sometimes even have an opposite effect, as when quality is identified with such statements as "I want this document off my desk in three hours," (because this is the norm). Obviously, we are no longer dealing with quality here, but with meeting standards or avoiding potential chastisement.

Standardization projects often demonstrate amazing naiveté, as if setting a standard will suddenly change people. Just as Gorbachev did not change the Soviet system by issuing a new decree, writing a quality manual will not change an organization's habits either. It takes more than that. This does not mean that quality manuals are useless or superfluous, it does mean, however, that the process of compiling such a "code" is at least as important as its contents. What is particularly naive is that this kind of approach often lacks the process element.

For every standard the question should be asked: "Is this a standard for or against something? Are we creating or avoiding something?" If standards are reactive, they will not be observed, for people will not see their usefulness. History teaches us that working on quality is a fundamental process that concerns everyone and is all about ways of seeing and thinking.

A survey into the similarities and differences of twelve Dutch Service Companies'[1] approaches to quality reveals that all approaches studied are different. No conclusions can be drawn about what generally will or will not work, or about what is the best approach. It appears that different approaches may all yield good results. The results of this study demonstrate that, fortunately, there are more ways than one to skin a cat. There is no standard way that is best for raising the level of quality-awareness in an organization.

Quality ceased being only "delivery in accordance with the specifications" or "fitness for use" or even "living up to expectations raised" a long time ago. Time and time again, we see that there is a "but" to every definition of what exactly constitutes quality. Each definition covers only part of what quality really is, and is therefore too restricted. For this reason, some organizations have chosen to work with what are called "critical quality characteristics," which do not define quality, but describe a number of characteristic aspects of it.

KLM Royal Dutch Airlines was mainly concerned with the aspects of reliability, punctuality, care and friendliness.

An administrative agency focused for a while on correctness, completeness, punctuality and comprehensibility.

The interesting thing about these examples is that they stress completely different quality aspects. KLM is apparently concerned with *virtues* in interpersonal relationships, while the administrative agency stresses *information*. The advantage of such an approach is that employees can be presented a clear image of how the company wants its customers to perceive it and how it wants to present itself on the market, indicating what is important and less important. It gives employees a number of focal points, something to go on. The disadvantage of such an approach is that it gives the impression that *this* is what quality must be, while quality signifies many other things as well. The "critical quality characteristics" approach seems to focus mainly on short-term results. The question of whether this is the best way to develop long-term quality awareness still remains open.

What Quality Really Is

Quality is essentially an expression of love: love for the customer, for one's fellow workers, for one's work and—last but not least—for oneself. In other words, underlying all quality problems are *relationship problems.* The degree to which leaders relate to their people will, to a large extent, determine the quality of their leadership. The degree to which team members relate to one another makes or breaks the quality of their co-operation. If the individual or the organization does not relate to the customer, the quality of service can only be low. The extent to which people relate to themselves and to others determines the quality of human interaction. If a person cannot relate to (the purpose of) his or her work, the quality of the work will suffer.

The concept of quality is meaningless without "relating." If relating is left out of the picture, quality programs are quite likely to degenerate into the writing of quality manuals and the setting of standards everyone must meet. If people can no longer relate to the standard (no longer regard it as an agreement that is logical and necessary), all vitality will disappear from the organization. In such cases, people should receive credit for using their creative powers to circumvent standards.

A sign of highly developed quality-awareness is when people behave as part of a larger whole, and let their actions be governed by the question of how to contribute best to this larger whole of which they are part. This kind of "process-orientation" has taken the place of the long-exalted "task-orientation." Task-oriented tunnel-vision is widened to a process-oriented perspective; the position has changed from a "me first" to a "win-win" attitude. The result is often that previous agreements (standards) are respected, although sometimes the result is that standards are anything but respected. Those who act with an eye to the whole organization will use their freedom of choice to make the best possible contribution to it. Highly developed quality-awareness prevents individual freedom of choice from degenerating into anarchy and chaos, and enriches the whole organization. In short, highly developed quality-awareness is one of the features of a creative organization.

Quality is a dynamic concept. That which is now considered "top quality service" may be perceived quite differently next year. The reason for this is the existence of different levels of quality.

1 *Compulsory quality.* This is the lowest (legally) acceptable quality; a lower level of quality is unthinkable and would threaten short-term continuity; systems and procedures ("It quality") often assure it.
2 *Expected quality.* This is the quality level expected by the customer, the standard that will have to be met to ensure long-term survival. This kind of quality is often linked to organizational culture ("We quality").
3 *Voluntary quality.* This is the kind of quality the customer does not expect, but certainly appreciates. It is that little bit extra, which gives the customer the feeling of not just being served, but being recognized and confirmed as a person. It is the more personal kind of quality ("I quality").

By providing unexpected but welcome quality (voluntary quality), you provide just that little bit extra that makes an organization stand out from the crowd. This high level must then be maintained to keep it from back-firing. As long as quality is not "put on" but is the result of an honest process of growth, based on love, there is no need to fear that it will relapse.

The three approaches to processes of change can also be applied to quality improvement.

Sometimes procedures and systems we work with every day stand in the way of quality. These can often be made more comprehensible and improved in such a way as to make them quicker, easier, simpler or more precise. Working on these systems and procedures is the most customary, traditional approach to quality improvement. One way to do this is by solving problems in project groups using simple analytical techniques, which often achieve visible and concrete results within a very short time.

Conducting a cultural analysis in order to reveal and discuss the existing culture can be an excellent approach for arousing interest in quality and reaching an agreement about what should be tackled first. A cultural analysis is a common starting point, particularly in those cases when there is no outside threat, because it makes it easy to connect up with what is going on inside the organization. The will to work on quality improvement can then be generated from inside.

The "We" approach most of all strengthens the "binding principle," the team spirit, making it easier for individuals to identify themselves with and relate to the organization of which they are a part.

Quality requires a personal leadership style to match every situation and every level of the organization. To bring the identity of his firm or department to life and keep it alive, to develop and spread a vision and a policy on quality, and to function as examples, as models: leaders must be able to do all of this. When they succeed, and it is far from easy, they become not just managers but inspiring leaders, who understand themselves and their core qualities as well as their co-workers and their core qualities. Such leaders can influence corporate culture and create the conditions for the success of a quality-improvement program.

Whichever of the three approaches is chosen as a starting point, sooner or later all three will become important; quality improvement always entails:

- Improving systems
- Improving the work climate
- Improving leadership

By redefining quality as a relationship problem, a sharp contrast is created with such approaches as Total Quality Management (TQM). TQM defines quality as consistent satisfaction of customer expectations. Anyone with any experience in quality programs for the service industry should realize this definition is nonsense, something you should not trouble your personnel with. By defining quality as consistent satisfaction of customer expectations, the customer is not only "always right," but taken to its extreme, even "almighty." Bringing such a definition into the organization is asking for trouble, and the employees' reaction is predictable: "So I am completely at the mercy of the customer! Thanks, but no thanks!"

Such an approach causes confusion and aversion to quality; the enthusiasm to work towards it disappears. A worse approach to starting a quality-awareness process could not possibly have been chosen. The management is immediately put on the defensive, because they have to explain that they did not mean it like that and all they wanted was stronger *customer-orientation*. This is their second mistake. If people are told they must become more customer-oriented, they will often interpret this as a reproach that they are being selfish, and perceive it as an attack on their integrity. Understandably, this provokes resistance. For this reason, customer-orientation is rarely a good opener for a quality program. This is borne out by cultural analyses: customer-orientation invariably scores highest of all categories, indicating that people usually act in a customer-oriented manner, or so they think. Whether they do or not is not really important. What matters is that this element rarely generates free energy. In other words, if management think this needs to be changed, they will have to come up with some hard facts, or everything they say will fall on deaf ears.

One of the most important issues of quality in service is learning how to *draw the line* and how to *make choices*. Customers expect and want something, as does the organization, for example to project a certain market image. In so doing, the organization (or the management) makes a choice to meet certain expectations and not to fulfill others. This choice is of particular importance in service industries, because it provides employees with guidelines for their actions. Within the chosen limits, every individual is free to impose his own limits and make his own choices.

The quality process takes us from a "rules-based culture" to an "agreement-based culture." Rules can be made one-sidedly, but it takes two parties to reach an agreement. Agreements can be changed, but not alone. Replacing a rule with an agreement implies recognition of mutual dependence and equality, quality generated from inside instead of imposed from outside.

Rules will always be necessary for an organization to function smoothly. These rules should focus mainly on compulsory quality and should be kept to a minimum. If a quality program is set up properly, people will end up formulating quality standards, simply out of a desire to maintain the high quality of their relationships. Standards are then generated from within and will be lived up to, or adapted if they are no longer relevant.

Quality and Congruence

An important element of the way creative organizations think about quality is the concept of "congruence:" the outside is a reflection of the inside. The quality that is outwardly visible to the customer is a reflection of internal quality. Whether departments treat each other as customers or not determines how the customer will eventually be treated. The inside and the outside must be congruous. This is true for the organization as a whole as well as for the departments, groups and—most of all—the individuals within it.

An individual is "congruous" with himself if his outward behavior is in harmony with his inner life. One of the prerequisites for "being congruous" is that you are in touch with yourself and able to face yourself, accepting both your good and your bad sides. In many organizations, the ability to appreciate and confront others, and therefore yourself, is underdeveloped. Quality improvement also entails paying attention to the personal development of individuals as described in Part One.

In summary, the conclusion can be drawn that the concept of quality needs rethinking, particularly in the service industries. Some of the aspects raised are:

- Quality is an issue involving relationships
- Quality means having the feeling of being part of a larger whole
- Quality results from an organic consciousness-raising process
- Quality requires congruence
- Quality can be assured in systems
- Quality must have its roots in people
- Quality can be approached in more ways than one
- Quality generates free energy
- Quality is an expression of … Love!

¹¹] Creativity

Why Creativity?

When talking about creative organizations, an obvious aspect to explore is how individual creativity can "enrich" the whole organization. Every organization has one or two people who are labeled "creative," the ones people consider to be maverick because they do things others cannot or dare not do. Although we do not know exactly what collective creativity is, we can say something about the factors influencing group creativity. We can start from the assumption that *Creativity* is influenced by *Quality* of thought on the one hand, and the *Climate* in a group on the other: $Cr = f(Q \times Cl)$.

Quality of thought depends on the ideas that are generated; you do not get far without creative ideas. Yet this is only half the story. Generally, the reason groups come up with few creative ideas can be found elsewhere; it is more a matter of climate. If the climate is "unsafe," people will think twice before expressing differing opinions. The way ideas are dealt with strongly influences the climate within a group. The greatest obstacle to creative solutions is that ideas are often treated as if they were solutions. This is caused by our way of thinking.

We tend to think in terms of good/bad, black/white, yes/no, beautiful/ugly etc. This way of thinking is called *decision thinking*. It is thinking in such opposites as: "Should I or shouldn't I?," "Do I go left or right?" It is either-or thinking, and we are well-trained in it. This kind of decision thinking makes us approach ideas as if they were already solutions. It is understandable that, when we look at a creative new idea in this way, we are almost bound to reject it as useless. It simply is not good enough yet, so we pick up another idea and subject it to the same critical scrutiny. So, most ideas that come up during brainstorming sessions will be rejected as undoable. Which is exactly why, in the past, people tended to say about brainstorming, "What's the point…" The lack of results was not due to brainstorming as a technique, but to the way the new ideas were handled. The point is that an *idea* is something different than a *solution*. An idea is the starting point of a process; the solution is the final result. To get from the starting point to the end, another way of thinking is needed, one that is called: *developmental thinking.*

Whereas decision thinking takes place in the left half of the brain, the right half is better at developmental thinking, thinking in terms of relations and associations, without judging utility or feasibility, good or bad. When somebody comes up with an idea, developmental thinking causes our reaction to move along the lines of:

"Let me think, what does that remind me of?"
"What other ideas does it evoke?"
"What does it suggest to me." And so on.

Developmental thinking can be clearly seen in small children who do not yet have a perfect command of the language. They learn mostly through developmental thinking, which may cause them to make the strangest connections. For example, when my two-year-old daughter was sitting on the counter the other day, watching me do the dishes, she said: "Look daddy… cup is taking a bath." In developmental thinking, it is normal to call a dishpan a bath, if a bath is all you know. So, cups take a bath. A bath also has soap and water, which would suggest that the dishpan the cups are washed in is also a bath.

We have unlearned developmental thinking because experience has taught us that it is (too) risky. Especially in environments that discouraged this kind of speculative thinking, we soon learned that we better do what the others do, which is to be certain that you are right before you open your mouth. This attempt to be "right" freezes part of our creativity. The unsafer the climate in a group, the more people will tend to censor their thoughts on the basis of "correctness," usually by asking questions. *Most questions are asked to test whether the thoughts we have in our heads are good enough and, consequently, whether we ourselves are good enough.* If the answer is negative, we reject the idea as irrelevant and so deprive others of the opportunity to add to it and improve it. Because who knows what people might think of when they hear my weird idea.

People in creative organizations have learned to take (calculated) risks, both in business and when it comes to expressing their ideas. Creativity will always flourish in groups with an open climate, a climate allowing a chain reaction to result eventually in new and creative solutions that no one could achieve on their own. To do this, we have to learn to react to ideas in a development-oriented way.

Characteristics of Creative Groups

Studies of successful groups show that creative solutions are found if groups:

- Do not let go of what they *do* want.
- Do not let themselves be held back by *ostensible* obstacles.
- Know how to reformulate obstacles so that they become challenges.
- Build on each other's ideas.

An effective way to do this is by making use of the *development reaction* (also called the "Itemized Response" in the Synectic method).

Imagine that you have a scale at the back of your mind: all the "useless" ideas fall on the left side of the scale, all the "perfect" ones on the right. It also has some kind of threshold of acceptance. The further right an idea is placed, the more valuable it is thought to be. Ideas to the left of the threshold of acceptance are often rejected (especially by decision thinking) as "not good enough."

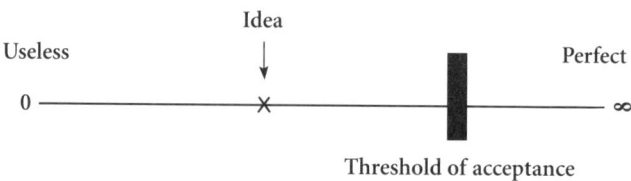

A developmental reaction means not reacting to the idea as a whole, but reacting to different aspects of it. We chop it up into pieces, as it were, and examine its different aspects separately. First we determine the attractive features of the idea:

- What part of this idea would we like to hold on to?
- What is challenging, meaningful or useful about the idea?
- Which direction does it point us in to find a possible solution?
- Which principles contained in the idea are usable?

This is not intended as an exercise in being nice to each other, but as a pointer towards success.

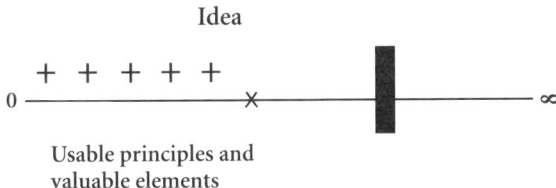

We subsequently determine the most important shortcomings that need to be worked on. The manner in which these are formulated is very important. If the problem is one of technical feasibility, for example, this could be formulated as an obstacle: "It's not do-able because it is technically impossible." We could also consider it a challenge, and then we would say "*How to* make it technically feasible."

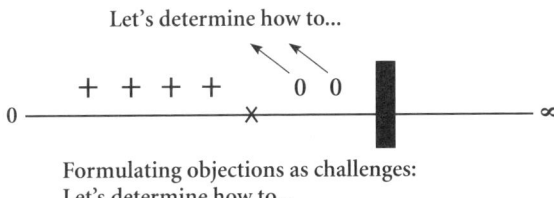

"This is impossible for my boss will never accept it" can be changed to: "How to make it acceptable to my boss." In this way, an obstacle is used to provide direction and progress, and the other person is invited to continue contributing ideas for solving the problem.

By converting objections into challenges, you engage in a kind of judo with ideas. All martial arts contain the principle of following the other's movements and then reversing them. If you brace yourself, you turn yourself into an obstacle and put yourself in a weak and vulnerable position.

It usually suffices to formulate the three most important objections; we do not need an exhaustive examination of all possible objections. That would be pointless, because the next idea is likely to be completely different.

When the most viable objection has been formulated, the group is invited to come up with *options* to the objection. An option can supplement an existing idea, bringing it closer to the threshold of acceptance, or it can be a completely new idea. In this phase, it is important to be able to let go of the original idea, if necessary.

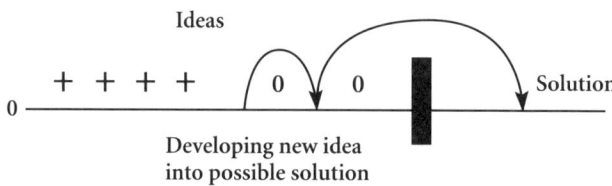

When you develop an idea, you have to retain the valuable aspects within it, but let the idea itself go. You take what it has to offer and use this to generate a new idea.

If developmental reaction becomes a normal way of working, and gets ingrained into the culture, this will have a number of significant ramifications. First of all, it will prevent people from becoming reactive and defensive, and help them to continue looking for possibilities in a creative fashion. Secondly, it creates a climate in which it is safe to express even half-baked ideas without fear of being tripped up, since every idea is judged on the basis of its merits. Finally, it increases the chances of ending up with creative solutions.

By creating an open climate like this, meetings will become more creative and productive. Much of the energy that is often unconsciously used to sound out and deliberate whether we can actually say something will now become available and can be channeled toward the task in hand.

It is not always advisable to use the developmental reaction. There are a number of pitfalls one should watch out for.

- Do not use the developmental reaction to try and argue that what is wrong is right. In other words, do not stick to an idea at all cost. Hold on to what is valuable in an idea, but let go of the idea itself.
- The developmental reaction can also be used as a moral weapon with which to "force" people to say something positive, but then it changes into: "You always have to think positively," while that is not the point.
- Occasionally a "problem owner" keeps raising new objections. *Objections are relevant only if they stop you from taking action.* Objections can be raised against many decisions, but as long as they do not prevent action from being taken, it does not really make sense to spend a great deal of time on it.
- Developmental reaction is not a substitute for problem *analysis.* Without thorough preparation and a problem analysis, it is not only very hard to provide direction, but objections will often be based on supposition instead of fact.
- When it comes to *action,* decision thinking is necessary. If you are crossing the street and a car is coming straight at you, there is no time to think about the attractive aspects or what it suggests to you. At that moment you must take action and make a decision.

Creativity in Creative Organizations

The development reaction can be studied at a number of levels. First of all, it can simply be considered as a handy *technique* which produces good results, reducing it to no more than a trump card, played mainly to evaluate ideas in creative problem solving meetings.

The developmental reaction can also be regarded as a *skill* that contributes to the creation of an open climate in which people are not afraid they will be punished for having chaotic ideas. Since both the specific advantages and disadvantages are listed, the person contributing the idea will probably experience his contribution (and as a result, himself) as valuable.

As a *strategy,* the developmental reaction prevents us from being sucked into a downward spiral of focusing only on why things are impossible, forbidden or wrong. The introduction of the development reaction can be a conscious strategy to teach the people in the organization to think in terms of possibilities, instead of impossibilities.

Finally, the development reaction reflects a mental attitude, a *philosophy* based on the principle that other people's ideas and work are valuable. A philosophy in which the will to contribute plays an important role.

In a creative organization, the same philosophy is recognizable at all levels and in all methods used:

- Direct your energy at something worthwhile, something that has growth potential and is possible.
- Be creative instead of reactive.
- Use setbacks or obstacles as signals to head you in the right direction.
- Know what you are in favor of, not what you are against.
- Choose what you want to create.

12] Against the Current?

The way things are
is not the real problem;
It is how we experience
things to be…

Time and Relativity

"Now! … now …!" the captain shouted.

I shot a quick glance at my watch and started paddling forward. Before I had rowed one stroke, my heart rate had gone up to 170. The first stroke was fine; the second barely skimmed the water. I was front-left on the raft. Two other paddlers sat behind me on the left side, the other three were on the right. The captain sat in the middle, towards the rear, and roared something I could no longer make out. The raft surged upwards, and on the fifth stroke I missed the water altogether and nearly lost my balance.

"Dig!…dig!…deeper!…harder…!"

I just managed to catch the commands my traveling companion repeated right behind me, because the noise of the water was deafening. The only thing I saw was water; the only thing I felt was this strange mixture of fear and excitement. My sunglasses were nearly wiped off my face by a wave that washed over me and left them dangling from the cord around my neck.

The violence surrounding me was overwhelming, towering waves were coming right at me.

"Left…Backwards!…left…backwards…!" the person behind me yelled. And instead of paddling forward, I threw my full weight into paddling backward.

Right in front of us, to the right, I saw an enormous whirlpool that looked like a ten-foot hole in the water. We barely missed it, but the force of the current hit the rubber raft and hurled it to the right. Fear turned to excitement.

About fifteen minutes earlier, when we had scouted the rapids and discussed the different passages and risks, it had become clear that we had to avoid the rock formation that lay to the right behind the whirlpool at all cost. As always, we had made a best-case scenario and a worst-case scenario and the latter sounded more than a little frightening. It was day twelve and these were the notorious Lavafalls rapids, the ones we feared most of all during our two-week rafting trip through the Grand Canyon. Bob, the captain, had told us about it over a week ago. In a sense, all the previous rapids had been leading up to this one.

The rocks came straight at me. We paddled backwards with all our might, the captain was hanging halfway overboard to help us make the turn to the left. I knew exactly what to do if the raft capsized. A bigger and more stable raft with a number of traveling companions had gone before, and we had seen how they had made it. They were waiting behind a rock on the edge of the river, ready to rescue any one from drowning, should one or more of us get into trouble.

"Nothing can happen," they had assured us. "If you get thrown out off the raft, make sure you keep your feet in front of you to cushion the impact in case you collide with a rock. Don't try to swim, that would be completely pointless. All you have to do is let yourself be carried along on your lifejacket and steer. If, in between waves, you get your head above water, take a quick lungful and keep your mouth shut under water. If you get into a whirlpool, don't fight it, just let yourself be dragged down, hold your breath and wait. It will never take longer than 30 seconds before it spits you out again. Everybody can hold their breath for 30 seconds anytime…"

This comforting message had carried us through a number of rapids. After discussing it with the captain, one time I had purposefully jumped overboard during our passage of one of the previous rapids, just to feel what it was like to be dragged along by the water while floating on your lifejacket; it was a fantastic experience. So, I had learned by now what the risks were.

Yet the actual confrontation was different. The rocks were right in the middle of our path and it was clear we would hit them. Or rather, I was convinced we would, it was just inevitable. The right side of the raft would crash into the rocks first. I realized I was glad to be on the left. Suddenly the raft seemed to drop down a few feet. Instead of being thrown to the right, we were tossed across the waves to the left. The back of the raft grazed the rocks.

"Forwards…!" the captain roared. I could hear his voice again. Every stroke of my paddle was "solid." It became less noisy and the captain shouted again: "Now…!" We had made it. I looked at the second hand of my watch and saw that just over 30 seconds had gone by. Out of breath and flabbergasted I kept staring at my watch. Thirty seconds… that was all. If someone had asked me how long it had taken, I would have sworn it had been 30 minutes. It seemed like an eternity, time had simply stood still. I knew that it was theoretically possible to live through so much in so little time, but I had never before experienced it as clearly as I did now.

Later, I wrote in my diary:

I knew we were going to crash on the rocks, but we didn't!
I knew there was no need to be afraid, and yet I was!
I knew for sure it must have lasted 30 minutes, yet it was only
    30 seconds!
I knew we were a team, yet all I could think of was myself!
Do I really know anything for sure?

And so the whole trip was one big confrontation with time and relativity. During our walks in the side canyons, time constantly stared at me from the rock faces. For 200,000,000 years this river has been flowing through the landscape, and in that time it has cut itself 5,500 feet into the earth's crust, creating the Grand Canyon. As I looked around me while we were out on the river, we seemed to be surrounded by mountains. In reality, the tops of these 5,500-feet peaks are the normal surface of the earth, and we were actually floating along at a depth of 5,500 feet inside the earth.

Every inch is 5,000 years! It took the river 5,000 years to cut one inch deeper into the earth, so during my lifetime it will wear down about one hundredth of an inch. One hundredth of an inch on 5,500 feet! And I get all worked up if I have to wait so much as an hour. My God, am I impatient!

Because I saw time enveloping me, I couldn't escape such questions as:

- What am I really doing?
- What is it all about?
- What does and does not upset me and why?
- Why am I on this planet?
- What are time and relativity?

These were the kind of questions that occupied me most during the trip. For the river, my two-week presence was but an insignificant moment in its history, for me it was an overwhelming experience.

Into the Current, Out of the Current

Being confronted with my fears is another experience I won't easily forget. While we were nearing the rapids and nothing had happened (yet), my pulse shot up to 170 out of fear for what might happen. This has absolutely nothing to do with the present reality, because in fact nothing has changed, but the prospect of approaching rapids makes the imagination run wild.

The same goes for making choices. Fear exists only in relation to the future, to time. Most striking of all was that, upon approaching the rapids, my fear kept growing, while it disappeared the moment I went in. As if the mind simply doesn't get the time to be afraid. There is no fear in the here and now! This jibed with what I had experienced when I had to make the most far-reaching choices of my life. If there was any fear to speak of, it was more a companion and a source of excitement and pleasure than a restraint.

"It's true that nothing can happen to you." That's to say, if I don't panic. The greatest dangers are not external but inside of myself. If I let my own panic confuse me and start gasping for air under water, things will go wrong. If I just hold my breath for a while, nothing will happen. This is not just true for the river, but for life as a whole. Fear of losing makes me lose. And it makes absolutely no difference whether this is fear of losing my life by drowning or losing my job because of the choices I make.

"If you are thrown overboard, do not try to swim, just steer." In situations when things start happening to me that I don't want, it is important that I keep steering, let myself be carried along and don't think

I can do it on my own. Have faith in the current, in life, that better times will surely come; learn to hold my breath, to breathe at the right moment, to endure, to not act for once and just let myself go with the flow.

The river had a new lesson to teach us every day. The river guides were very well aware of the fact that their only role was to act as facilitators. "Think of the river as your teacher…" was the first thing they told us when we got on board. As a teacher, the river had a great deal of wisdom to impart to us.

At times, the river was so wide and so quiet that you could hardly see whether it was flowing, and if so, where; sometimes it was on the left, sometimes in the middle, and then suddenly it was on the right. When I, as steersman, lost contact with the current and drifted beside it, it took extra paddling to make headway. That meant putting the crew to work to correct my "mistake." To the others, a good steersman meant they could relax. A good leader was one who was in tune with the current. Then the least energy was wasted. Talking about leadership…!

Sometimes it was hard not to feel guilty about and blame myself for my limited capacity to "sense" the current. That is something I also come across in my daily work as a consultant or process manager. If I do not sense a group process correctly, the group usually will have to work harder.

The raft sometimes passed an eddy, a slowly circling current at the edge of the river, going round in an endless circle (of no less than 60 feet across). Everything that gets caught up in it, can circle endlessly. You can see bits of driftwood going round and round that may have been in there for months or even years. It requires an enormous effort on the part of the whole crew to break free from an eddy and return to the current. If you look at it from a distance, it is hard to imagine how difficult it is to get out of an eddy. It's incredibly hard work.

The interesting thing about eddies was that if I closed my eyes, it felt as if I was in the middle of the stream and going forwards, while in fact we even went backwards now and then. I wondered how often my own life is caught up in an eddy, while I am under the impression that I am making headway. How often haven't I pursued success, worked like a madman and cherished the illusion that I was doing great? How many people live their lives circling in an eddy, under the impression they are making progress while they have actually stopped growing? To what extent is a career the eddy many men are caught up in?

I remembered the effort it took me at various points in my life to get back on the right track again, back onto the current. I certainly could not have done it alone, and I was grateful for the help given me by all my friends and helpers who had paddled along with me through my life.

Creating in and on the Current would also have been a good title for this book…

Silence and Reflection

The most impressive moments were those of silence and peace. Often, hours would pass without anyone saying a word. While we were paddling, or during our walks in the side canyons to waterfalls straight out of Eden, we only spoke if we really had something to say. At the beginning of the trip we had agreed to be aware of when we said something and why. "Let the silence be silent, unless you have something to say…" I have never been in a group where so little was said, and yet I have never communicated more efficiently than during those two weeks.

Now, a few years later, I often have moments that I relive part of this trip of inspiration. The moment we returned to the river bank for the last time after two weeks, and said good-bye to the river with a slight bow— something we had done at the end of every day—I could see myself sitting behind my desk in my office, recalling the image of the river. At that moment, I internalized the river, as it were. I knew that for the rest of my life I had found an inner guide that would always be there. Every time I have to make a fundamental choice or decision and join my inner self with the river current, I touch upon a more profound knowledge that surpasses my personal wishes and concerns.

All I have to do is just be quiet, do nothing and listen. It is so close that I often wonder why I persist in using it so little.

Appendix 1] The Earth Charter

For over a decade diverse groups throughout the world have endeavored to create an Earth Charter that sets forth fundamental ethical principles for a sustainable way of life. As a result of a worldwide consultation process, the Earth Charter Commission issued a final version of the Earth Charter after their meeting on March 12–14, 2000 at the UNESCO headquarters in Paris.

The Earth Charter is a declaration of interdependence and responsibility and an urgent call to build a global partnership for sustainable development. The principles of the Earth Charter are closely interrelated. Together they provide a conception of sustainable development and set forth fundamental guidelines for achieving it. These principles are drawn from international law, science, philosophy, religion, recent un Summit meetings, and the international Earth Charter conversation on global ethics.

PREAMBLE

We stand at a critical moment in Earth's history, a time when humanity must choose its future. As the world becomes increasingly interdependent and fragile, the future at once holds great peril and great promise. To move forward we must recognize that in the midst of a magnificent diversity of cultures and life forms we are one human family and one Earth community with a common destiny. We must join together to bring forth a sustainable global society founded on respect for nature, universal human rights, economic justice, and a culture of peace. Towards this end, it is imperative that we, the peoples of Earth, declare our responsibility to one another, to the greater community of life, and to future generations.

Earth, Our Home

Humanity is part of a vast evolving universe. Earth, our home, is alive with a unique community of life. The forces of nature make existence a demanding and uncertain adventure, but Earth has provided the conditions essential to life's evolution. The resilience of the community of life and the well-being of humanity depend upon preserving a healthy biosphere with all its ecological systems, a rich variety of plants and animals, fertile soils, pure waters, and clean air. The global environment with its finite resources is a common concern of all peoples. The protection of Earth's vitality, diversity, and beauty is a sacred trust.

The Global Situation

The dominant patterns of production and consumption are causing environmental devastation, the depletion of resources, and a massive extinction of species. Communities are being undermined. The benefits of development are not shared equitably and the gap between rich and poor is widening. Injustice, poverty, ignorance, and violent conflict are widespread and the cause of great suffering. An unprecedented rise in human population has overburdened ecological and social systems. The foundations of global security are threatened. These trends are perilous—but not inevitable.

The Challenges Ahead

The choice is ours: form a global partnership to care for Earth and one another or risk the destruction of ourselves and the diversity of life. Fundamental changes are needed in our values, institutions, and ways of living. We must realize that when basic needs have been met, human development is primarily about being more, not having more. We have the knowledge and technology to provide for all and to reduce our impacts on the environment. The emergence of a global civil society is creating new opportunities to build a democratic and humane world. Our environ-

mental, economic, political, social, and spiritual challenges are inter-
connected, and together we can forge inclusive solutions.

Universal Responsibility

To realize these aspirations, we must decide to live with a sense of universal
responsibility, identifying ourselves with the whole Earth community as
well as our local communities. We are at once citizens of different nations
and of one world in which the local and global are linked. Everyone shares
responsibility for the present and future well-being of the human family
and the larger living world. The spirit of human solidarity and kinship
with all life is strengthened when we live with reverence for the mystery of
being, gratitude for the gift of life, and humility regarding the human
place in nature.

We urgently need a shared vision of basic values to provide an ethical
foundation for the emerging world community. Therefore, together in
hope we affirm the following interdependent principles for a sustainable
way of life as a common standard by which the conduct of all individuals,
organizations, businesses, governments, and transnational institutions is
to be guided and assessed.

PRINCIPLES

RESPECT AND CARE FOR THE
COMMUNITY OF LIFE

1 **Respect Earth and life in all its diversity.**
a Recognize that all beings are interdependent and every form of life has
  value regardless of its worth to human beings.
b Affirm faith in the inherent dignity of all human beings and in the
  intellectual, artistic, ethical, and spiritual potential of humanity.

2 **Care for the community of life with understanding, compassion, and
  love.**
a Accept that with the right to own, manage, and use natural resources

comes the duty to prevent environmental harm and to protect the rights of people.

b Affirm that with increased freedom, knowledge, and power comes increased responsibility to promote the common good.

3 Build democratic societies that are just, participatory, sustainable, and peaceful.

a Ensure that communities at all levels guarantee human rights and fundamental freedoms and provide everyone an opportunity to realize his or her full potential.

b Promote social and economic justice, enabling all to achieve a secure and meaningful livelihood that is ecologically responsible.

4 Secure Earth's bounty and beauty for present and future generations.

a Recognize that the freedom of action of each generation is qualified by the needs of future generations.

b Transmit to future generations values, traditions, and institutions that support the long-term flourishing of Earth's human and ecological communities.

In order to fulfill these four broad commitments, it is necessary to:

ECOLOGICAL INTEGRITY

5 Protect and restore the integrity of Earth's ecological systems, with special concern for biological diversity and the natural processes that sustain life.

a Adopt at all levels sustainable development plans and regulations that make environmental conservation and rehabilitation integral to all development initiatives.

b Establish and safeguard viable nature and biosphere reserves, including wild lands and marine areas, to protect Earth's life support systems, maintain biodiversity, and preserve our natural heritage.

c Promote the recovery of endangered species and ecosystems.

170

d Control and eradicate non-native or genetically modified organisms harmful to native species and the environment, and prevent introduction of such harmful organisms.

e Manage the use of renewable resources such as water, soil, forest products, and marine life in ways that do not exceed rates of regeneration and that protect the health of ecosystems.

f Manage the extraction and use of non-renewable resources such as minerals and fossil fuels in ways that minimize depletion and cause no serious environmental damage.

6 **Prevent harm as the best method of environmental protection and, when knowledge is limited, apply a precautionary approach.**

a Take action to avoid the possibility of serious or irreversible environmental harm even when scientific knowledge is incomplete or inconclusive.

b Place the burden of proof on those who argue that a proposed activity will not cause significant harm, and make the responsible parties liable for environmental harm.

c Ensure that decision making addresses the cumulative, long-term, indirect, long distance, and global consequences of human activities.

d Prevent pollution of any part of the environment and allow no build-up of radioactive, toxic, or other hazardous substances.

e Avoid military activities damaging to the environment.

7 **Adopt patterns of production, consumption, and reproduction that safeguard Earth's regenerative capacities, human rights, and community well-being.**

a Reduce, reuse, and recycle the materials used in production and consumption systems, and ensure that residual waste can be assimilated by ecological systems.

b Act with restraint and efficiency when using energy, and rely increasingly on renewable energy sources such as solar and wind.

c Promote the development, adoption, and equitable transfer of environmentally sound technologies.

d Internalize the full environmental and social costs of goods and services in the selling price, and enable consumers to identify products that meet the highest social and environmental standards.

e Ensure universal access to health care that fosters reproductive health and responsible reproduction.

f Adopt lifestyles that emphasize the quality of life and material sufficiency in a finite world.

8 **Advance the study of ecological sustainability and promote the open exchange and wide application of the knowledge acquired.**

a Support international scientific and technical cooperation on sustainability, with special attention to the needs of developing nations.

b Recognize and preserve the traditional knowledge and spiritual wisdom in all cultures that contribute to environmental protection and human well-being.

c Ensure that information of vital importance to human health and environmental protection, including genetic information, remains available in the public domain.

SOCIAL AND ECONOMIC JUSTICE

9 **Eradicate poverty as an ethical, social, and environmental imperative.**

a Guarantee the right to potable water, clean air, food security, uncontaminated soil, shelter, and safe sanitation, allocating the national and international resources required.

b Empower every human being with the education and resources to secure a sustainable livelihood, and provide social security and safety nets for those who are unable to support themselves.

c Recognize the ignored, protect the vulnerable, serve those who suffer, and enable them to develop their capacities and to pursue their aspirations.

10 **Ensure that economic activities and institutions at all levels promote human development in an equitable and sustainable manner.**

a Promote the equitable distribution of wealth within nations and among nations.

b Enhance the intellectual, financial, technical, and social resources of developing nations, and relieve them of onerous international debt.

c Ensure that all trade supports sustainable resource use, environmental protection, and progressive labor standards.

d Require multinational corporations and international financial organizations to act transparently in the public good, and hold them accountable for the consequences of their activities.

11 **Affirm gender equality and equity as prerequisites to sustainable development and ensure universal access to education, health care, and economic opportunity.**

a Secure the human rights of women and girls and end all violence against them.

b Promote the active participation of women in all aspects of economic, political, civil, social, and cultural life as full and equal partners, decision makers, leaders, and beneficiaries.

c Strengthen families and ensure the safety and loving nurture of all family members.

12 **Uphold the right of all, without discrimination, to a natural and social environment supportive of human dignity, bodily health, and spiritual well-being, with special attention to the rights of indigenous peoples and minorities.**

a Eliminate discrimination in all its forms, such as that based on race, color, sex, sexual orientation, religion, language, and national, ethnic or social origin.

b Affirm the right of indigenous peoples to their spirituality, knowledge, lands and resources and to their related practice of sustainable livelihoods.

c Honor and support the young people of our communities, enabling them to fulfill their essential role in creating sustainable societies.

d Protect and restore outstanding places of cultural and spiritual significance.

13 Strengthen democratic institutions at all levels, and provide transparency and accountability in governance, inclusive participation in decision making, and access to justice.

a Uphold the right of everyone to receive clear and timely information on environmental matters and all development plans and activities which are likely to affect them or in which they have an interest.

b Support local, regional and global civil society, and promote the meaningful participation of all interested individuals and organizations in decision making.

c Protect the rights to freedom of opinion, expression, peaceful assembly, association, and dissent.

d Institute effective and efficient access to administrative and independent judicial procedures, including remedies and redress for environmental harm and the threat of such harm.

e Eliminate corruption in all public and private institutions.

f Strengthen local communities, enabling them to care for their environments, and assign environmental responsibilities to the levels of government where they can be carried out most effectively.

14 Integrate into formal education and life-long learning the knowledge, values, and skills needed for a sustainable way of life.

a Provide all, especially children and youth, with educational opportunities that empower them to contribute actively to sustainable development.

b Promote the contribution of the arts and humanities as well as the sciences in sustainability education.

c Enhance the role of the mass media in raising awareness of ecological and social challenges.

d Recognize the importance of moral and spiritual education for sustainable living.

15 Treat all living beings with respect and consideration.

a Prevent cruelty to animals kept in human societies and protect them from suffering.

b Protect wild animals from methods of hunting, trapping, and fishing that cause extreme, prolonged, or avoidable suffering.

c Avoid or eliminate to the full extent possible the taking or destruction of non-targeted species.

16 **Promote a culture of tolerance, nonviolence, and peace.**

a Encourage and support mutual understanding, solidarity, and co-operation among all peoples and within and among nations.

b Implement comprehensive strategies to prevent violent conflict and use collaborative problem solving to manage and resolve environmental conflicts and other disputes.

c Demilitarize national security systems to the level of a non-provocative defense posture, and convert military resources to peaceful purposes, including ecological restoration.

d Eliminate nuclear, biological, and toxic weapons and other weapons of mass destruction.

e Ensure that the use of orbital and outer space supports environmental protection and peace.

f Recognize that peace is the wholeness created by right relationships with oneself, other persons, other cultures, other life, Earth, and the larger whole of which all are a part.

THE WAY FORWARD

As never before in history, common destiny beckons us to seek a new beginning. Such renewal is the promise of these Earth Charter principles. To fulfill this promise, we must commit ourselves to adopt and promote the values and objectives of the Charter.

This requires a change of mind and heart. It requires a new sense of global interdependence and universal responsibility. We must imaginatively develop and apply the vision of a sustainable way of life locally, nationally, regionally, and globally. Our cultural diversity is a precious heritage and different cultures will find their own distinctive ways to realize the vision. We must deepen and expand the global dialogue that generated the Earth Charter, for we have much to learn from the ongoing collaborative search for truth and wisdom.

Life often involves tensions between important values. This can mean difficult choices. However, we must find ways to harmonize diversity with unity, the exercise of freedom with the common good, short-term objectives with long-term goals. Every individual, family, organization, and community has a vital role to play. The arts, sciences, religions, educational institutions, media, businesses, nongovernmental organizations, and governments are all called to offer creative leadership. The partnership of government, civil society, and business is essential for effective governance.

In order to build a sustainable global community, the nations of the world must renew their commitment to the United Nations, fulfill their obligations under existing international agreements, and support the implementation of Earth Charter principles with an international legally binding instrument on environment and development.

Let ours be a time remembered for the awakening of a new reverence for life, the firm resolve to achieve sustainability, the quickening of the struggle for justice and peace, and the joyful celebration of life.

More information: www.earthcharter.org

Appendix 2] The Genetic Code of Kern Konsult

Simplicity is the experience of Unity…

The Genetic Code of Kern Konsult is a document for in-house use written by and for the firm's employees and networkers, in which the firm's identity and values have been set down. Its contents are constantly honed and fine-tuned.

Kern Konsult

Kern Konsult was conceived in June 1984 and born in January 1985. The vision that resulted in the inception of Kern Konsult, is set down in our declaration of principles, which was formulated in the fall of 1984. Laying down our principles provides us with a touchstone for our comings and goings, our thinking and our actions.

We call this document the Genetic Code of Kern Konsult. It verbalizes the soul of Kern Konsult as a living organism. The Genetic code is the constant factor in the firm's life, in which cells can change, divide and renew themselves. The outward form may change, but the core remains the same, no matter who the people involved are. The Genetic Code of Kern Konsult provides a sense of *identity*, on the one hand, and an indication of what *values* are important, on the other. It also provides a sense of *direction,* of looking ahead, the idea that all of today's actions are an investment in the future.

The genetic code's three elements are:

- Identity
- Values
- Direction

This piece is about those three elements, about the identity, values and direction of Kern Konsult.

Identity

To be able to recognize Kern Konsult's identity, we will first have to get to know it, that is, learn to find it. In this process of searching, the emphasis is first of all on the process, not the result. Our identity is partly revealed by the way we work in and regard organizations, and how we treat our clients. On this subject, our declaration of principle says the following:

- We believe an organization is a living organism with a task that is both internal and external.
- To perform this task, the organization has potential qualities.
- We want to help the organization and the people in it to make these Core Qualities productive.
- We want people to put their heart and soul into what they do.
- We want to work in a practical and result-oriented way.

These few lines express our identity and reveal us to the outside world.

By saying an organization is a *living organism,* we say that we will treat it as such; with respect for life and in search of the (healing) power within the organism itself, interested mainly in health and vitality, a situation in which profit is a result rather than a goal in itself. A healthy organism is characterized by *rhythm* and *balance,* where action and rest, decisiveness and patience, inhaling and exhaling all have their time and place. This way of thinking and seeing things shapes our identity. We are not management consultants in the traditional sense; we do not immediately disappear after having written a report and investigated a company. We are not so much surgeons as natural healers. With everything we do we ask ourselves: How does this enhance the organization's vitality? What we do is release energy.

Why? To enable the organization to fulfill its *task, both internally and externally.* We feel an organization does not simply exist, it has an essential contribution to make, not only to the well-being of its shareholders and employees, but also to the well-being of its clients and social environment.

The purpose (or the sense) of every organization is to contribute to the well-being of the larger whole of which it is a part. So, we are always concerned with questions of meaning. That is a constituent of the Genetic Code of Kern Konsult.

Another feature of our identity or approach is that we trust an organism's *potential core qualities* to help the organization help itself. This attitude is unassuming only in the sense that we do not pretend to know all the answers. Our strength lies in asking the right questions, so that people can formulate their own answers. We are not reorganizers, but process designers. We will not easily tell our clients (neither management nor employees) how to do things better or differently. That's something the clients themselves usually know best.

When we say we want to allow people to *put their heart into it,* we mean we want to help them relate to what the organization stands for from within themselves, so that the organization's objectives and their personal goals are synchronized. This means learning to do what you have to do with love, out of free will and without sacrificing yourself.

We let Respect, Integrity and Love determine what we do. This is manifested in our inner and outward attitude towards individuals and organizations, expressing that:

> *You can be as you are*
> *to become who you are,*
> *but cannot yet be;*
> *and you can become this*
> *in your own way*
> *and in your own good time.*

And finally, when we say we want to work in a *practical and result-oriented* manner, we express that we both recognize and accept that our vision and ideas are of value only, insofar as they lead to practical results in everyday cooperation, on the basis of the motto that Work is Love in Action.

Values

Another vital part of our genetic code, besides identity, is comprised by our values. By formulating values, we make it possible to test our actions. They provide us with a touchstone for what is important.

Kern Konsult stands for *quality*. Quality is an expression of Love. Whatever we do, we give our all, regardless of the nature or importance of the client, or the fee we receive. This requires precision, thoroughness and skill, so we only do things we have *feeling* for, things we have an *understanding* of. Quality is not just doing what the client expects. Sometimes, quality is actually giving the client what he does not expect. Most important of all is the question: is there a *relation*? Quality is making clear to the client what he can expect from us, and once we have come to an agreement about it, meeting his expectations 100 percent.

A second important value we cherish is *congruence:* the harmony between inside and outside. Inside and outside mirror each other. This goes for each of us individually, and for Kern Konsult as a whole. What we say and do must "jibe," we do not compromise on this point. That is why private life and working life cannot be separated, and why it will always be important to work on our personal development. "Congruence" demands the utmost of each of us.

The third touchstone for our actions is *creativity,* in the sense of being creative instead of reactive. A creative attitude requires us constantly to ask: what are we in favor of, instead of what we are opposed to. Reactive behavior is revealed in the desire to avoid or escape difficult situations. Innovation is closely linked to creativity. We are trendsetters, pioneers in the field of organizations. New concepts and ideas are our lifeblood, they demand an open climate and an open mind, responsiveness to feedback and an open ear. And again: inside and outside should mirror each other.

The fourth value we foster is *meaningful growth,* qualitative growth. What we do should contribute to life and to a regenerative world. We are more concerned with regeneration and less with improvement. Outward growth is never our goal; it is the result and reflection of inner growth, which again is the result of accepting responsibility. We subscribe to the Declaration of Human Responsibilities.

The purpose of these values is not primarily external; they are internal guidelines for our actions and thoughts. Each of us is responsible for guarding these values and can be called to account about them the moment they join Kern Konsult.

Direction

Identity and value lead to direction. Kern Konsult is a firm of consultants that is rather different than most, because what we basically do is express movement. We talk of quality from within, or leadership from within. The essence of this movement is that it comes *from within,* and it is from within that it seeks to contribute to the evolution of our planet. It is a movement towards wholeness. That movement is Kern Konsult's direction. The forms we will choose may change, the essence of the organism that is Kern Konsult is laid down in the Genetic Code.

This document is an expression of that.

May we live and work in accordance with the privilege of our responsibility, which we hereby take upon us.

Noten]

Chapter 1 – Introduction

1 Peter Russell, "The Global Brain," video-tape based on his book *The Awakening Earth: Our Next Evolutionary Leap*. Ark Paperbacks, 1984.

2 Prof. Dr. C.J. Zwart, "Leiderschap en organisatie op de drempel van de toekomst," Hein Stufkens, Chapter 1 of *Management voor een nieuwe tijd*, (Lemniscaat, 1986).

3 Cees Swarttouw, "Het Transformatieparadigma," Hein Stufkens, Chapter 2 of *Management voor een nieuwe tijd*, (Lemniscaat, 1986).

4 "Introducing the Findhorn Foundation," video-tape (1989) released by the Visual Arts Department, Findhorn Foundation, The Park, Forres IV36 OTZ, Scotland.

5 Dr. Robert W. Terry, "Leadership – A preview of a seventh view," Reflective Leadership Program 1987, Humphrey Institute of Public Affairs, Minneapolis.

6 Prof. Ir. C.H. Botter, *Industrie en organisatie*. Kluwer, 1974.

Chapter 2 – Core Qualities

1 Kenneth Blanchard & Spencer Johnson, *The One Minute Manager*. Berkley Publishing Group.

2 Hans Korteweg, Hanneke Korteweg-Frankenhuisen, Jaap Voigt, *De grote Sprong*. Servire 1990.

3 Paul Hersey & Kenneth Blanchard, *Management of Organizational Behavior: Utilizing Human Resources*. Englewood Cliffs N.J.: Prentice-Hall, 1982.

4 Roger Harrison, "Leiderschap en strategische planning in een nieuwe tijd," Chapter 4 of John Adams' book *Transformatie* (Lemniscaat 1986).

Chapter 3 – Wishing versus Choosing

1 Robert Fritz, *The Path of Least Resistance: Learning to Become the Creative Force in Your Own Life*. Fawcett Books, 1990.

2 Steven Levine, *Meetings at the Edge*. Anchor Books Doubleday, 1988.

3 Elizabeth Kübler-Ross, *Life Lessons*.

Chapter 4 – Who Actually Chooses?

1 Roberto Assagioli M.D., *The Act of Will*. Wildwood House, 1973.

2 Piero Ferrucci, *What We May Be: Techniques for Psychological and Spiritual Growth Through Psychosynthesis.* Turnstone Press, 1982.

3 Carl Jung, "Two Essays on Analytical Psychology," (London, 1928).

4 Roberto Assagioli, *Psychosynthesis: A Manual of Principles and Techniques.* Turnstone Books, 1965).

5 M.A. Visintainer, J.R. Volpicelli, M.E.P. Seligman, "Tumor Reaction in Rats after Inescapable and Escapable Shock," *Science*, 1982.

Chapter 5 – The Developing Organization

1 Roger Harrison: "Leiderschap en strategische planning in een nieuwe tijd," Chapter 4 of John Adams' book *Transformatie*, Lemniscaat 1986.

2 Roger Harrison, "Understanding your organization's character," *Harvard Business Review*, (May/June 1972).

3 Ganzevoort, J., "Organisatie-ideologieën," *Intermediair*, 1981, p. 13–21).

4 Handy, C.B., *Gods of Management: The Changing Work of Organizations.* Kluwer 1981.

Chapter 8 – From a Reactive Organization to a Creative One

1 Linda Nelson and Frank L. Burns, "Topprestatie-programmering: een schema voor de transformatie van organisaties." Chapter 9 of John Adams' book *Transformatie*, Lemniscaat 1986).

2 Huub Vinkenburg, *Dienen of Verdienen.* Kluwer.